رَوْضَةُ التَّجْوِيدِ

بسم الله الرحمن الرحيم

In the name of Allah, the Entirely Merciful, the Especially Merciful.

All praise is due to Allah, Lord of the Worlds.

Peace and blessings be upon Muḥammad, Mercy to all Mankind.

رَوْضَةُ التَّجْوِيْد

Rawḍat at-Tajwīd

Intermediate Level Tajwīd for Students of Knowledge

Based on the Urdu textbook by

Qāriʾ Zakirhusen

Translated and adapted by the staff of

Markazul Uloom (Girls)

Blackburn, UK

Al Waraq

First Edition March 2017

ISBN 978-1-912193-00-4

Published by:

Al Waraq Publications

alwaraq@mugirls.org.uk

tinyurl.com/alwaraq

Distributed by:

Markazul Uloom (Girls)
Park Lee Rd
Blackburn
BB2 3NY

info@mugirls.org.uk

(+44) 1254 581 569

Printed in Great Britain by Islamic Printing, Blackburn

sales@islamicprinting.co.uk

اقْرَأْ وَارْتَقِ وَرَتِّلْ كَمَا كُنْتَ تُرَتِّلُ فِي الدُّنْيَا

Read and ascend, and recite beautifully, the way you used to recite in the world...

For Sheereen Apa

who first introduced me to the World of Tajwīd

May Allah grant you peace and happiness in both worlds

and ease the burdens of both

May you be showered with His Blessings

enlightened by His Nūr

and protected under His Shade

the day there is no shade except His

Āmīn

Transliteration Key

ء (أ إ)	’	A glottal stop, like when an English person drops the *t* in words such as *sat* and *pot*.
	’	Used to indicate where a hamzat al-waṣl has been dropped from the beginning of a word, e.g. in *dāru ’s-salām*.
ا	a, ā	
ب	b	
ت	t	
ث	th	Pronounced as the *th* in *thin* or *thirst*.
ج	j	
ح	ḥ	Tensely breathed *h* sound.
خ	kh	Pronounced like the *ch* in the Scottish *loch* with the mouth hollowed to produce a full sound.
د	d	
ذ	dh	Pronounced as the *th* in *this* or *that*.
ر	r	
ز	z	
س	s	
ش	sh	
ص	ṣ	A heavy *s* pronounced with the mouth hollowed to produce a full sound.

ض	ḍ	A heavy *d* pronounced with the mouth hollowed to produce a full sound.
ط	ṭ	A heavy *t* pronounced with the mouth hollowed to produce a full sound.
ظ	ẓ	A heavy *dh* pronounced with the mouth hollowed to produce a full sound.
ع	‘	A guttural sound, pronounced from the throat, which can be likened to the sound at the beginning of a gulp.
غ	gh	Pronounced like a throaty French *r* (but incorporating *g* sound) with the mouth hollowed to produce a full sound.
ف	f	
ق	q	A guttural *q* sound with the mouth hollowed to produce a full sound.
ك	k	
ل	l	
م	m	
ن	n	
ه	h	
و	w, ū	
ي	y, ī	

Contents

Editor's preface

بِسْمِ اللهِ الرَّحْمٰنِ الرَّحِيْمِ. اَلْحَمْدُ لِلّٰهِ وَكَفٰى وَسَلَامٌ عَلٰى عِبَادِهِ الَّذِيْنَ اصْطَفٰى.

Rawḍat at-Tajwīd is an intermediate-level tajwīd guide aimed at students who have already grasped the basics of tajwīd and will be able to absorb the more technical aspects.

The presentation of the Qur'ānic text in this book is broadly in line with the 'South African' 13-line Qur'ān, with a few notable exceptions. For example, the *hamzah aṣlīyah* is displayed as it would be in the Arabian muṣḥaf (copy): an alif with a small hamzah above or below it.[1]

Also, we have given preference to Arabic terms over their corresponding Urdu variations. For example, you will find that the 'alif maddah', as it is commonly known in Urdu, has been referred to as *alif maddīyah*.

There are many ways of reciting the Qur'ān, the discussion of which is unfortunately out of our scope. Nevertheless, the tajwīd rules explained in this book are in accordance with the riwāyah (narration) of Imām Ḥafs ﷺ, who is the student of Imām 'Āṣim ﷺ, who recited in the ṭarīqah (way) of 'Allāmah ash-Shāṭibī ﷺ.

Some chapters contain small exercises/extension tasks to help students consolidate their knowledge of tajwīd theory in different ways; teachers could use these ideas and develop them further, according to their students' needs.

Please note: if you are a novice, *Rawḍat at-Tajwīd* **must** be studied under the practical guidance of a tajwīd expert; tajwīd is an oral science, and cannot be mastered by simply studying the written theory!

If a person does not have access to a teacher for a valid reason, they should listen to qurrā' (reciters) such as Shaykh Maḥmūd Khalīl al-

---

[1] In fact, along the long road of adapting and editing this book, we have found that the script in the Arabian muṣḥaf is very beneficial when used to recognise and implement various tajwīd rules. Readers should certainly explore this avenue if they have become proficient at reciting in the South African print.

Ḥuṣarī رحمه الله, Shaykh Muḥammad Siddīq al-Minshāwī رحمه الله, Shaykh ʿAbd al-Basiṭ ʿAbd aṣ-Ṣamad رحمه الله, Shaykh ʿAlī ibn ʿAbd ar-Raḥmān al-Ḥudhayfī, etc. and try to learn from their recitation until they find a suitable teacher.

They should first listen intently to the sounds of the letters and try to practise them, using the makhārij and ṣifāt sections in this book to help them understand how to pronounce each letter. Next, they should study the rest of the tajwīd rules, and try to match them with what they are hearing in the recordings of these qurrāʾ.

This is also good practice for those who have previously learnt tajwīd, but are not quite up to scratch, or those who are already learning with a teacher, but would like further practice.

For those teachers or students who understand Arabic, one other very beneficial source of guidance is Shaykh Ayman Rushdī Suwayd, a Syrian scholar whose comprehensive explanations of tajwīd rules have been uploaded by third parties onto YouTube.

Finally, all good is from Allah عز وجل and all mistakes in content are ours alone. If you spot any errors or have any suggestions for improvement, please email alwaraq@mugirls.org.uk; we will endeavour to make any relevant changes for the next edition, in shāʾ Allah.

Free resources are available from our webpage: tinyurl.com/alwaraq.

We pray that Allah عز وجل accepts this humble offering, and makes us from amongst those who *read and ascend* on the Day of Reckoning. Āmīn.

M Hajee

Faculty of Tajwīd, Markazul Uloom (Girls), Blackburn

Jumāda l'-Ukhrā, 1438 (March, 2017)

Author's introduction

بِسْمِ اللهِ الرَّحْمٰنِ الرَّحِيْم. نَحْمَدُهُ وَ نُصَلِّيْ عَلٰى رَسُوْلِهِ الْكَرِيم.

In the Name of Allah, the Entirely Merciful, the Especially Merciful. We praise Him, and send salutations upon His Noble Messenger.

Reading and teaching the Noble Qurʾān with tajwīd is necessary for every Muslim. The Prophet ﷺ emphasised its importance in the following ḥadīth:

خَيْرُكُمْ مَنْ تَعَلَّمَ الْقُرْآنَ وَعَلَّمَهُ (رواه البخاري)

'The best of you is he who learns the Qurʾān and teaches it (to others).'

It is necessary to learn and understand the rules of tajwīd in order to recite the Qurʾān in the correct manner.

Many great scholars have written books on the subject of tajwīd; for example, *Fawāʾid Makkīyah* by Qāriʾ ʿAbd ar-Raḥmān Makkī ؒ and *Jamāl al-Qurʾān* by Mawlāna Ashraf ʿAlī Thānvī ؒ, amongst countless others written in Urdu. Many makātib and madāris are benefitting from these publications.

I thus present to you this small book (Rawḍat at-Tajwīd) written on the same subject, in which the rules of tajwīd are written in a simple and concise manner.

If this book is studied and taught in the correct manner, then we will be saved from this warning:

رُبَّ قَارِئٍ لِلْقُرْآنِ وَالْقُرْآنُ يَلْعَنُهُ (إحياء علوم الدين)

'There are many who recite the Qurʾān, yet the Qurʾān curses them.'

May Allah ﷻ honour this book with His acceptance, and make its benefits reach far and wide. Āmīn.

(Qāriʾ) Zakirhusen

Darul Uloom Al-Arabiya Al-Islamiya, Bury

بسم الله الرحمن الرحيم

اَلْحَمْدُ لِلّٰهِ الَّذِىْ مَنَّ عَلٰى مَنْ شَاءَ مِنْ عِبَادِهٖ بِحِفْظِ كِتَابِهٖ وَجَعَلَهٗ مُحَافِظًا عَلَى التَّجْوِيْدِ وَأَحْكَامِهٖ وَأَنَارَ قُلُوْبَ عِبَادِهٖ بِنُوْرِهٖ وَهُدَاهُ وَشَرَّفَنَا بِخِدْمَتِهٖ وَنَشْرِ عُلُوْمِهٖ. وَالصَّلَاةُ وَالسَّلَامُ عَلٰى خَيْرِ عِبَادِهٖ وَرُسُلِهٖ سَيِّدِنَا مُحَمَّدٍ وَعَلٰى آلِهٖ وَأَصْحَابِهِ الَّذِيْنَ غَاصُوْا فِىْ أَعْمَاقِ الْقُرْآنِ وَأَبْرَزُوْا أَسْرَارَهٗ وَنَشَرُوْا تَعْلِيْمَهٗ وَرَفَعُوْا مَنَارَهٗ وَعَلٰى مَنْ تَبِعَهُمْ مِنَ الْقُرَّاءِ الْمُجَوِّدِيْنَ إِلٰى يَوْمِ الْقِيَامَةِ.

All praise to Allah who bestowed whomever He willed amongst his servants with the memorisation of His book, and made him (the ḥafiẓ) a preserver of tajwīd and its rules; and enlightened the hearts of His servants with its light and its guidance; and honoured us with its service and the spreading of its knowledge.

Blessings and peace be upon the best of His servants and messengers, our leader Muḥammad; and upon his family and his companions, who dived into the depths of the Qur᾿ān and brought out its secrets, spread its teachings and raised high its banner; and (peace and blessings) upon those who follow them amongst the Qurrā᾿ al-Mujawwidīn[2], until the Day of Judgement.

Chapter 1: Etiquettes and virtues of the Qur᾿ān

Etiquettes of reading the Qur᾿ān

The etiquettes of reciting the Qur᾿ān can be divided into two types: inner and outer.

The inner qualities are:

1. **Acknowledgment of the source of the speech**, i.e. Allah عَزَّ وَجَلَّ, and His immense favour and mercy in addressing mankind and making it easy for mankind to understand His speech.
2. **Recognition of His greatness**, and that what is being recited is not from the speech of man, but the words of the Almighty عَزَّ وَجَلَّ.

[2] Those who recite the Qur᾿ān whilst adhering to all the rules of tajwīd.

3. **Presence of the heart** – to cease any personal thoughts or daydreaming during tilāwah.
4. **Deep contemplation** – for there is no benefit in reciting without thought; the servant must carry out the commandments of His Lord after understanding and pondering over them.
5. **Thorough understanding** – so that the right conclusions can be made after reading each verse.
6. **Taking every word as a special and personal address from Allah** عَزَّوَجَلَّ, i.e. to read the Qur'ān like a subject would read a letter from his king, paying special attention to the king's orders and prohibitions.
7. **Being truly affected by reading each verse** – to become happy at the mention of Jannah, fearful at the mention of Jahannam, humbled when reading about the qualities and magnificence of Allah عَزَّوَجَلَّ, etc.
8. **Ascension in status due to recitation** – so that the more a person recites, the higher their rank is elevated.
9. **Abandoning any practices that will prevent understanding**, e.g. to focus solely on tajwīd, to persist in sinning, to have love for the world in the heart, etc.
10. **Keeping free from pride and arrogance** – the reciter must avoid thinking highly of their own self, e.g. that they are pure from sin, or mighty and powerful.

The outer rules of conduct are to:

- Correct the intention; read seeking only the pleasure of Allah عَزَّوَجَلَّ, and for reward in the hereafter.

- Recite in the state of wuḍū᾽; the muṣḥaf (copy of the Qur᾽ān) or Qur᾽ānic verses written on any surface[3] must not be touched without wuḍū᾽.
- Clean the mouth with a miswāk, apply perfume, and wear nice clothes.
- Sit with dignity and tranquillity in a clean and respectful place, facing the qiblah if possible.
- Recite the Qur᾽ān with tartīl[4] and tajwīd; bearing in mind the rules of taʿawwudh and tasmiyah, waqf and waṣl, etc.
- Recite the Qur᾽ān loudly in a melodious voice, as long as others are not disturbed and there is no possibility of showing off; do not recite in a tune that sounds like singing.
- Recite the Qur᾽ān in the chapter order of the muṣḥaf.
- Be conscious of reciting the words of Allah ﷻ; do not talk of worldly things whilst reciting the Qur᾽ān.
- Close the Qur᾽ān if the need arises to talk; do not leave it open whilst not in use.
- Recite with emotion; learn the meaning of the Qur᾽ān from an authentic source to assist your understanding and emotion.
- Cry with sadness and emotion; if you cannot cry out of sadness, cry over the hardness of your heart.

---

[3] If the Qur᾽ānic text is displayed on an electronic device (such as a smartphone), do not touch the area of the screen displaying the Qur᾽ānic verses without wuḍū᾽. However, it will be permissible to touch the rest of the device without wuḍū᾽, according to the majority of scholars.

[4] To recite correctly and clearly. Allah ﷻ says in the Qur'ān: وَرَتِّلِ الْقُرْآنَ تَرْتِيلًا which means 'And recite the Qur'ān with measured recitation' [73:4]. Tartīl is the method of recitation to achieve the pleasure of Allah ﷻ. Tajwīd is the tool to master tartīl.

- Ponder over the meaning of the verses and practice the teachings of the Qur᾿ān.
- Recite the Qur᾿ān daily, even if it is in small amounts.
- Memorise as much of the Qur᾿ān as possible.
- Keep the Qur᾿ān in a respectful place – not on the floor, or where people sit. Do not place items on top of it.

Some aḥādīth on the virtues of the Qur᾿ān

عن عائشة رضي الله عنها قالت، قال رسول الله صلى الله عليه وسلم: اَلَّذِيْ يَقْرَأُ الْقُرْآنَ وَهُوَ مَاهِرٌ بِهِ مَعَ السَّفَرَةِ الْكِرَامِ الْبَرَرَةِ، وَالَّذِيْ يَقْرَأُ الْقُرْآنَ وَيَتَتَعْتَعُ فِيْهِ وَهُوَ عَلَيْهِ شَاقٌّ لَهُ أَجْرَانِ.

ʿĀ᾿ishah ﵂ narrates that the Messenger of Allah ﷺ said: *The one who recites the Qur᾿ān and is proficient in its recitation will be with the honourable and obedient scribes (angels), and the one who recites the Qur᾿ān and stammers and it is difficult for him will gain a double reward.* [Bukhārī and Muslim]

عن أبي موسى رضي الله عنه عن النبي صلى الله عليه وسلم، قال: تَعَاهَدُوْا هٰذَا الْقُرْآنَ فَوَالَّذِيْ نَفْسُ مُحَمَّدٍ بِيَدِهِ لَهُوَ أَشَدُّ تَفَلُّتًا مِنَ الإِبِلِ فِيْ عَقْلِهَا.

Abu Mūsā Al-Ashʿarī ﵁ narrates that the Prophet ﷺ said: *Commit yourselves to this Qur᾿ān, because, by the One in Whose Hand Muḥammad's soul is, it escapes (from memory) faster than a camel does from its ropes.* [Bukhārī and Muslim]

عن أبي أمامة رضي الله عنه، قال سمعت رسول الله صلى الله عليه وسلم يقول: اِقْرَءُوا الْقُرْآنَ فَإِنَّهُ يَأْتِيْ يَوْمَ الْقِيَامَةِ شَفِيْعًا لِأَصْحَابِهِ.

Abū Umāmah ﵁ narrates that I heard the Messenger of Allah ﷺ say: *Read the Qur᾿ān, for it will come on the Day of Resurrection as an intercessor for its reciters.* [Muslim]

وعن أبي هريرة رضي الله عنه، قال قال رسول الله صلى الله عليه وسلم: مَا اجْتَمَعَ قَوْمٌ فِيْ بَيْتٍ مِنْ بُيُوْتِ اللهِ يَتْلُوْنَ كِتَابَ اللهِ وَيَتَدَارَسُوْنَهُ بَيْنَهُمْ، إِلَّا نَزَلَتْ عَلَيْهِمُ السَّكِيْنَةُ وَغَشِيَتْهُمُ الرَّحْمَةُ وَحَفَّتْهُمُ الْمَلَائِكَةُ وَذَكَرَهُمُ اللهُ فِيمَنْ عِنْدَهُ.

Abū Hurayrah ﵁ narrates that the Messenger of Allah ﷺ said: *A group of people do not assemble in one of the houses of Allah to recite the Qurʾān and study it together, except that tranquillity will descend upon them, mercy will engulf them, the angels will surround them and Allah will make mention of them to those (the angels) in His proximity.* [Muslim]

وعن عبد الله بن عمرو بن العاص رضي الله عنهما عن النبي صلى الله عليه وسلم، قال: يُقَالُ لِقَارِئِ الْقُرْآنِ: اِقْرَأْ وَارْتَقِ وَرَتِّلْ كَمَا كُنْتَ تُرَتِّلُ فِي الدُّنْيَا، فَإِنَّ مَنْزِلَتَكَ عِنْدَ آخِرِ آيَةٍ تَقْرَؤُهَا.

ʿAbdullah ibn ʿAmr ﵄ narrates that the Prophet ﷺ said: *It will be said (on the Day of Judgement) to the reciter of the Qurʾān, 'Read and ascend (in rank), and recite the way you used to recite in the world, for indeed your place (in Jannah) will be at the last verse you recite.'* [Abū Dāwūd and Tirmidhī]

وعن ابن مسعود رضي الله عنه، قال قال رسول الله صلى الله عليه وسلم: مَنْ قَرَأَ حَرْفًا مِنْ كِتَابِ اللهِ فَلَهُ حَسَنَةٌ، وَالحَسَنَةُ بِعَشْرِ أَمْثَالِهَا، لَا أَقُوْلُ الٓمٓ حَرْفٌ، وَلٰكِنْ أَلِفٌ حَرْفٌ وَلَامٌ حَرْفٌ وَمِيْمٌ حَرْفٌ.

ʿAbdullah ibn Masʿūd ﵁ narrates that the Messenger of Allah ﷺ said: *Whoever recites a letter from the Book of Allah, he will be credited with a good deed, and a good deed gets a ten-fold reward. I do not say that Alif-Lām-Mīm is one letter, but alif is a letter, lām is a letter and mīm is a letter.* [Tirmidhī]

Exercise: Make a poster or presentation detailing the inner and outer etiquettes of reciting the Qurʾān, and present your work to your study group or class.

Chapter 2: What is tajwīd?

Literal meaning of tajwīd: to make something better or to improve it.

Technical definition of tajwīd: to pronounce the Arabic letters from their correct places (makhārij), along with their permanent and temporary qualities (ṣifāt).

The subject of tajwīd: the ḥurūf al-hijāʾ (Arabic alphabet).

The aim of tajwīd: to recite the Qurʾān correctly, according to the way of the Prophet ﷺ, as narrated by the scholars of tajwīd through the ages.

It is evident from many narrations that the Prophet ﷺ used to take care in articulating every letter clearly and correctly from its place when reciting the Qurʾān. He ﷺ used to pause (make waqf) in suitable places and have special regard in elongating the madd and pronouncing the letters correctly and beautifully.

It is wājib (necessary) for the reciters of the Qurʾān to implement the rules of tajwīd in their recitation.

Exercise: Find a Qurʾānic verse or ḥadīth that shows the importance of reciting the Qurʾān in a beautiful manner, and memorise it.

Chapter 3: Major and minor errors

If the Qur᾿ān is not recited with tajwīd, then this is known as *laḥn*. Laḥn means 'mistake'. There are 2 types of laḥn:

1. Laḥn Jalīy
2. Laḥn Khafīy

Al-laḥn al-jalīy اللَّحْنُ الجَلِيّ

Literal meaning: clear error. These are major errors, which include:

1) Pronouncing one letter as another (see *Appendix 1)*, e.g.

اَلْحَمْدُ as اَلْهَمْدُ

2) Reading one ḥarakah as another (see *Appendix 1)*, e.g.

الْمُرْسَلِيْنَ as الْمُرْسِلِيْنَ

3) Reading a sākin[5] as a mutaḥarrik[6] or vice versa, e.g.

آمَنْتُ as آمَنَتْ

أَنَعْمْتَ / أَنْعَمَتَ instead of أَنْعَمْتَ

4) Neglecting such a ṣifah that differentiates one letter from another, e.g. neglecting the ṣifah of isti῾lā᾿ (full mouth) and reading

صَابِرِيْنَ as سَابِرِيْنَ

Not pronouncing the ṣād with isti῾lā᾿ will make it sound like a sīn.

5) Adding a letter to a word, e.g.

---

[5] A letter with a sukūn (ْ◌) on it.

[6] A letter with a ḥarakah on it.

اَلْحَمْدُوْ لِلّٰه instead of اَلْحَمْدُ لِلّٰه

6) Removing a letter from a word, e.g.

لَمْ يَلَدْ as لَمْ يُوْلَدْ

It is ḥarām (forbidden) to make laḥn jalīy whilst reciting the Qurʾān, and the person who does this will be sinful; it is a major sin.

Al-laḥn al-khafīy اللَّحْنُ الخَفِيّ

Literal meaning: hidden error. These are minor errors, which include:

1) Neglecting such a ṣifah of which the sole purpose is to enhance the beauty of the letter that is pronounced.

   For example: neglecting ikhfāʾ, madd, or ghunnah, or not pronouncing the tafkhīm/tarqīq in the lām of الله or the letter rā.

2) Neglecting such a ṣifah that is not a differentiator between two letters, i.e. a ṣifah that does not distinguish between one letter and another.

   For example: neglecting a madd, or reciting a strong qalqalah as a weak one.

It is makrūh (disliked) to make laḥn khafīy whilst reciting the Qurʾān; it is a minor sin.

Exercise: Choose a partner and recite a few verses of the Qurʾān to each other. Note down any mistakes, and decide whether they are laḥn jalīy or khafīy.

Chapter 4: The types of recitation

There are 3 types of tilāwah (recitation):

1. Taḥqīq
2. Ḥadr
3. Tadwīr

At-taḥqīq التَّحْقِيْق

Literal meaning: to fulfill something meticulously (without any shortfalls or excess).

Technical definition: to recite slowly in such a way that every letter is pronounced separately and clearly.

Al-ḥadr الحَدْر

Literal meaning: to descend with speed, to express quickly (an utterance or thought).

Technical definition: rapid recitation of the Qur'ān (in comparison to taḥqīq).

Please note that despite the speed of recitation, it is necessary to properly pronounce the makhraj, ṣifah and ḥarakah of every single letter.

At-Tadwīr التَّدْوِير

Literal meaning: to spin or turn around.

Technical definition: recitation of the Qur'ān at medium speed, between taḥqīq and ḥadr.

> **Exercise:** Go online and find audio clips representing each of the three types of recitation. Alternatively, demonstrate each type under the supervision of your teacher.

Chapter 5: Istiʿādhah and basmalah

Reciting istiʿādhah (taʿawwudh) and basmalah (tasmiyah) before the recitation of the Qurʾān is established from the Qurʾān.

Al-istiʿādhah الاِسْتِعَاذَة / التَّعَوُّذ

فَإِذَا قَرَأْتَ الْقُرْآنَ فَاسْتَعِذْ بِاللهِ مِنَ الشَّيْطٰنِ الرَّجِيمِ

So, when you recite the Qurʾān, seek refuge with Allah against Shayṭān, the Accursed [16:98]

Literal meaning of istiʿādhah: to seek refuge.

It is necessary to recite istiʿādhah at the beginning of a recitation. The best words of istiʿādhah are أَعُوْذُ بِاللهِ مِنَ الشَّيْطٰنِ الرَّجِيم (known as Taʿawwudh ar-Rasūl). Istiʿādhah may also be recited using other words, such as أَعُوْذُ بِاللهِ السَّمِيْعِ الْعَلِيْمِ مِنَ الشَّيْطٰنِ الرَّجِيم, but the first option is better.

Istiʿādhah differentiates between the Holy Qurʾān and other books, therefore it is makrūh to read istiʿādhah before starting other (non-Qurʾānic) texts. At the beginning of other texts, e.g. durūd or duʿāʾ, only tasmiyah may be recited.

Al-basmalah البَسْمَلَة / التَّسْمِيَة

إِقْرَأْ بِاسْمِ رَبِّكَ

Read in the name of your Lord [96:1]

Meaning of basmalah: to recite بِسْمِ اللهِ الرَّحْمٰنِ الرَّحِيْم.

The basmalah is a verse of the Qurʾān that is written and recited before every sūrah, and it separates one sūrah from another.

It is necessary to recite the basmalah before starting any sūrah. The only exception is Sūrat at-Tawbah (also known as Sūrat al-Barāʾah), which is in Juzʾ 10. Whether the reciter starts recitation from the beginning of

Sūrat at-Tawbah, or finishes Sūrat al-Anfāl and then goes on to read Sūrat at-Tawbah, they must not recite the basmalah before commencing Sūrat at-Tawbah.

Some rules of isti'ādhah and basmalah

- If recitation is commenced from the *middle* of a sūrah (whether this is Sūrat at-Tawbah or otherwise), there is a choice whether or not to read the basmalah – however, it is better to do so.

  If basmalah is not recited, it is permissible to do waṣl[7] between isti'ādhah and the verse, e.g.

  أَعُوْذُ بِاللهِ مِنَ الشَّيْطٰنِ الرَّجِيمِ ذٰلِكَ الْكِتَابُ لَا رَيْبَ فِيْهِ

  Please note that when the verse starts with Allāh's name, waqf must be made between isti'ādhah and the verse[8], e.g.

  اَللّٰهُ لَآ إِلٰهَ إِلَّا هُوَ　　　　اَلرَّحْمٰنُ عَلَى الْعَرْشِ اسْتَوىٰ

  It is incorrect to say: أَعُوْذُ بِاللهِ مِنَ الشَّيْطٰنِ الرَّجِيمِ اللّٰهُ لَآ إِلٰهَ إِلَّا هُوَ

- When reciting loudly or in the presence of an audience, isti'ādhah should be recited aloud as well.

- During the recitation, if the reciter coughs, sneezes or talks about something regarding the recitation or the tafsīr (explanation) of the

---

[7] Waṣl is to join without making a pause, e.g. joining the isti'ādhah to the verse without stopping.

[8] Imām ash-Shāṭibi ﷺ used to order the recitation of basmalah after isti'ādhah when beginning recitation at اَللّٰهُ لَآ إِلٰهَ إِلَّا هُوَ or إِلَيْهِ يُرَدُّ عِلْمُ السَّاعَةِ due to the offensiveness of linking shayṭān's qualities to Allah ﷻ. Based on this, the reciter should refrain from reciting basmalah when commencing with a verse that begins with shayṭān's name or mention, e.g. اَلشَّيْطٰنُ يَعِدُكُمُ الْفَقْرَ or لَعَنَهُ اللّٰهُ due to the offensiveness of linking Allah's sublime qualities to shayṭān.

verse, then repeating the istiʿādhah before resuming the recitation is not necessary.

- If the reciter talks about an unrelated matter (something not connected to the verses they are reciting) during recitation, or replies to a salām, then reciting istiʿādhah before resuming is necessary.

  Similarly, if the reciter sneezes whilst reciting, and thereafter utters 'Al-ḥamdu li 'llāh!', they must repeat the istiʿādhah.

- If, after performing a waqf[9], the reciter conducts another activity or changes majlis (gathering)[10], istiʿādhah will be necessary before resuming recitation.

  If the recitation is continuous whilst the reciter changes majlis or carries out an activity, there will be no need for istiʿādhah.

Exercise: Make a chart or mind-map summarising the information above, i.e. when istiʿādhah and basmalah are necessary, recommended or forbidden.

---

[9] Waqf is to pause recitation, with the intention of resuming straight after.

[10] Changing places, getting up and joining another group of people, leaving the room, or entering a different room, are all examples of what would constitute a change of gathering.

Chapter 6: Ways of beginning recitation

Important terms

1. **Waṣl al-kull:** full continuation, e.g. to join the istiʿādhah, basmalah and verse.

2. **Faṣl al-kull:** full separation, e.g. to separate the istiʿādhah, basmalah and verse.

3. **Waṣl al-awwal wa faṣl ath-thānī:** continuation of the first part and separation of the second, e.g. to join the istiʿādhah and basmalah, and read the verse separately.

4. **Faṣl al-awwal wa waṣl al-thānī:** separation of the first part and continuation of the second, e.g. to read the istiʿādhah separately, and join the basmalah and verse.

Three ways of beginning recitation

1. Beginning a recitation at the start of a sūrah; in this case, reciting the istiʿādhah and basmalah is necessary.

There are 4 ways in which this can be done, and all 4 are correct:

✓ **وَصْلُ الْكُلّ:** أَعُوْذُ بِاللهِ مِنَ الشَّيْطٰنِ الرَّجِيْمِ بِسْمِ اللهِ الرَّحْمٰنِ الرَّحِيْمِ الْحَمْدُ لِلّٰهِ رَبِّ الْعٰلَمِيْن

✓ **فَصْلُ الْكُلّ:** أَعُوْذُ بِاللهِ مِنَ الشَّيْطٰنِ الرَّجِيْم [وقف] بِسْمِ اللهِ الرَّحْمٰنِ الرَّحِيْم [وقف] اَلْحَمْدُ لِلّٰهِ رَبِّ الْعٰلَمِيْن

✓ **وَصْلُ الأَوَّلِ وَفَصْلُ الثَّانِي:** أَعُوْذُ بِاللهِ مِنَ الشَّيْطٰنِ الرَّجِيْمِ بِسْمِ اللهِ الرَّحْمٰنِ الرَّحِيْم [وقف] اَلْحَمْدُ لِلّٰهِ رَبِّ الْعٰلَمِيْن

✓ **فَصْلُ الأَوَّلِ وَوَصْلُ الثَّانِي:** أَعُوْذُ بِاللهِ مِنَ الشَّيْطٰنِ الرَّجِيْم [وقف] بِسْمِ اللهِ الرَّحْمٰنِ الرَّحِيْمِ الْحَمْدُ لِلّٰهِ رَبِّ الْعٰلَمِيْن

2. Beginning a recitation from the middle of a sūrah; in this case, istiʿādhah is necessary and basmalah is optional.

Out of the four ways of doing this, two are correct (*faṣl al-kull* and *waṣl al-awwal wa faṣl ath-thānī*) and two are incorrect (*waṣl al-kull* and *faṣl al-awwal wa waṣl ath-thānī*):

- ✗ **وَصْلُ الْكُلّ**: أَعُوْذُ بِاللهِ مِنَ الشَّيْطٰنِ الرَّجِيْمِ بِسْمِ اللهِ الرَّحْمٰنِ الرَّحِيْمِ ذٰلِكَ الْكِتَابُ لَا رَيْبَ فِيْه

- ✓ **فَصْلُ الْكُلّ**: أَعُوْذُ بِاللهِ مِنَ الشَّيْطٰنِ الرَّجِيْم [وقف] بِسْمِ اللهِ الرَّحْمٰنِ الرَّحِيْم [وقف] ذٰلِكَ الْكِتَابُ لَا رَيْبَ فِيْه

- ✓ **وَصْلُ الأَوَّلِ وَفَصْلُ الثَّانِي**: أَعُوْذُ بِاللهِ مِنَ الشَّيْطٰنِ الرَّجِيْمِ بِسْمِ اللهِ الرَّحْمٰنِ الرَّحِيْم [وقف] ذٰلِكَ الْكِتَابُ لَا رَيْبَ فِيْه

- ✗ **فَصْلُ الأَوَّلِ وَوَصْلُ الثَّانِي**: أَعُوْذُ بِاللهِ مِنَ الشَّيْطٰنِ الرَّجِيْم [وقف] بِسْمِ اللهِ الرَّحْمٰنِ الرَّحِيْمِ ذٰلِكَ الْكِتَابُ لَا رَيْبَ فِيْه

Waṣl al-kull is not permitted here because it is the middle of a sūrah and basmalah is not necessary, only optional.

Also waṣl al-awwal wa faṣl ath-thānī is not permitted here because it will then seem like the basmalah is part of the sūrah, i.e. someone might think it is the beginning of a sūrah.

3. Beginning a sūrah in the middle of a recitation; in this case, basmalah is necessary.

Out of the four ways of doing this, three are correct (*waṣl al-kull*, *faṣl al-kull* and *faṣl al-awwal wa waṣl ath-thānī*) and one is incorrect (*waṣl al-awwal wa faṣl ath-thānī*):

✓ **وَصْلُ الْكُلّ:** غَيْرِ الْمَغْضُوْبِ عَلَيْهِمْ وَلَا الضَّآلِّيْنَ بِسْمِ اللهِ الرَّحْمٰنِ الرَّحِيْمِ الٓمّٓ ذٰلِكَ الْكِتَابُ لَا رَيْبَ فِيْه

✓ **فَصْلُ الْكُلّ:** غَيْرِ الْمَغْضُوْبِ عَلَيْهِمْ وَ لَا الضَّآلِّيْن [وقف] بِسْمِ اللهِ الرَّحْمٰنِ الرَّحِيْم [وقف]الٓمّٓ ذٰلِكَ الْكِتَابُ لَا رَيْبَ فِيْه

× **وَصْلُ الْأَوَّلِ وَفَصْلُ الثَّانِي:** غَيْرِ الْمَغْضُوْبِ عَلَيْهِمْ وَلَا الضَّآلِّيْنَ بِسْمِ اللهِ الرَّحْمٰنِ الرَّحِيْم [وقف]الٓمّٓ ذٰلِكَ الْكِتَابُ لَا رَيْبَ فِيْه

✓ **فَصْلُ الْأَوَّلِ وَوَصْلُ الثَّانِي:** غَيْرِ الْمَغْضُوْبِ عَلَيْهِمْ وَلَا الضَّآلِّيْن [وقف] بِسْمِ اللهِ الرَّحْمٰنِ الرَّحِيْمِ الٓمّٓ ذٰلِكَ الْكِتَابُ لَا رَيْبَ فِيْهِ

Waṣl al-awwal wa faṣl ath-thānī is not permitted here because there is a risk of assuming that the basmalah is the final verse of the previous sūrah.

Summary table	**Waṣl al-kull**	**Faṣl al-kull**	**Waṣl al-awwal wa faṣl ath-thānī**	**Faṣl al-awwal wa waṣl ath-thānī**
Beginning a recitation at the start of a sūrah	✓	✓	✓	✓
Beginning a recitation from the middle of a sūrah	×	✓	✓	×
Starting a sūrah in the middle of a recitation	✓	✓	×	✓

Chapter 7: Makhārij

Literal meaning of makhraj (plural – makhārij): place of exit.

Technical definition: place from where the sound of a letter is articulated.

Neglecting to pronounce a letter from its correct makhraj is a laḥn jalīy.

To recognise the exact makhraj of a letter, it should be read as a sākin preceded by an alif maftūḥah (bearing in mind the rules given below for each letter); the place where the sound ends is the makhraj. E.g. For the letter qāf, vocalise أَقْ aloud in order to discern its exact makhraj[11].

According to Imām Ibn al-Jazarī ﷾, there are 17 makhārij, as follows (each makhraj is numbered in bold):

Ḥurūf al-madd حُرُوْفُ الْمَدّ / الْحُرُوْفُ الْهَوَائِيَّة

1. The makhraj of the ḥurūf al-madd (or ḥurūf hawā'īyah) is the *jawf al-famm wal ḥalq* (the empty place in the mouth and throat).

There are three ḥurūf al-madd, which can easily be remembered by the word نُوْحِيْهَا:[12]

Alif[13] maddīyah: when the letter before an alif has a fatḥah (◌َ) on it, e.g.

إِحْدَاكُمْ   عَادَيْتُمْ   بَا تَا ثَا

---

[11] Take care not to use parts of the mouth that are not specified within the descriptions of each makhraj; tips and common mistakes will be outlined in the footnotes.

[12] The alif, wāw or yā' in the ḥurūf al-madd will not be pronounced as though they have a hamzah or sukūn on them, e.g. by pronouncing نُوْحِيْهَا as nuw-ḥiy-ha', instead of nū-ḥī-hā (in nuw-ḥiy-ha', the w, y and ' sounds are pronounced, which is incorrect). Similarly, the ḥurūf al-madd must not be pronounced as though they have a hamzah *after* them, e.g. by saying nū'-ḥī'-hā'.

[13] Please note that alif is free of all ḥarakāt and sukūn. When an alif gets a sukūn or a ḥarakah, it is known as a hamzah.

Wāw maddīyah: when the letter before a wāw sākinah has a ḍammah (ُ◌) on it, e.g.

أُوْ بُوْ تُوْ أَخْرَجُوْكُمْ قَتَلُوْكُمْ

Yāʾ maddīyah: when the letter before a yāʾ sākinah has a kasrah (ِ◌) under it, e.g.

إِیْ بِیْ تِیْ بِإِيْمَانِهِمْ فِيْهِمْ

Al-ḥurūf al-ḥalqīyah الْحُرُوْفُ الْحَلْقِيَّة

These are known as the ḥurūf ḥalqīyah because they are pronounced from the *ḥalq* (throat):

2. The makhraj of ء and ه is the aqṣa ʻl-ḥalq, i.e. the bottom of the throat.

3. The makhraj of ع and ح is the wasaṭ al-ḥalq, i.e. the middle of the throat.[14]

4. The makhraj of غ and خ is the adna ʻl-ḥalq, i.e. the top of the throat.[15]

Al-ḥurūf al-lahawīyah الْحُرُوْفُ اللَّهَوِيَّة

These are known as the ḥurūf lahawīyah because they are pronounced near the *lahāh* (uvula), which is a piece of flesh that hangs between the mouth and throat.

---

[14] When pronouncing ḥāʾ and ʿayn, such force should not be imposed on the throat, that the head moves and the listener thinks that they are being forcibly pronounced; they should be pronounced in a refined manner.

[15] The pronunciation of the khāʾ and ghayn should not be exaggerated so as to cause repetition (of the letter sound). Avoid the unpleasant 'getting ready to spit' sound!

5. The makhraj of ق: the upper part of the back of the tongue touches the corresponding part of the upper palate.

6. The makhraj of ك: the lower part of the back of the tongue touches the corresponding part of the upper palate.

The makhraj of kāf is near the makhraj of qāf, but slightly closer to the front of the mouth.

Al-ḥurūf ash-shajrīyah الحُرُوْفُ الشَّجْرِيَّة

The ḥurūf shajrīyah are pronounced from the *shajr al-famm* (area between the middle of the tongue and the upper palate).

7. The makhraj of ج, ش, ياء مُتَحَرِّكَة and ياء اللِّيْن: the middle of the tongue touches the corresponding part of the upper palate.

Al-ḥarf al-ḥāfī الحَرْفُ الحَافِي

This letter is known as the ḥarf ḥāfī because it is pronounced from the *ḥāfat al-lisān* (side edges of the tongue).

8. The makhraj of ض: the upturned sides of the tongue touch the roots of the corresponding top molars.

Al-ḥurūf adh-dhalqīyah الحُرُوْفُ الذَّلْقِيَّة / الحُرُوْفُ الطَّرَفِيَّة

These are known as ḥurūf dhalqīyah (or ḥurūf ṭarafīyah) because they are pronounced from the front edge (commonly referred to as the 'tip') of the tongue. *Dhalq* and *ṭaraf* both mean 'tip' or 'point'.

9. The makhraj of ل: the tip of the tongue touches the gums of the top front teeth, from premolar to premolar.

10. The makhraj of ن: the tip of the tongue touches the gums of the top front teeth, from canine to canine.

11. The makhraj of ر: the tip of the tongue touches the gums of the upper central and lateral incisors.

Al-ḥurūf an-niṭʿīyah الحُرُوْفُ النِّطْعِيَّة

These are known as the ḥurūf niṭʿīyah because they are pronounced from the *niṭʿ* (hard palate, i.e. the roots of the upper central incisors).

12. The makhraj of ط, د and ت: the tip of the tongue touches the roots of the upper central incisors.

Al-ḥurūf al-asalīyah الحُرُوْفُ الْأَسَلِيَّة / حُرُوْفُ الصَّفِيْر

These are known as the ḥurūf asalīyah because they are pronounced from the sharp tip of the tongue. *Asalah* means the 'tip of the tongue', and its root word also carries the meaning of 'sharpening'. They are also known as ḥurūf aṣ-ṣafīr, i.e. the 'letters of the whistle'.

13. The makhraj of ص, س and ز: the tip of the tongue, the edges of the upper central incisors and the lower central incisors all meet together.[16]

Al-ḥurūf al-lithawīyah الحُرُوْفُ اللِّثَوِيَّة

These are known as the ḥurūf lithawīyah because they are pronounced from the teeth that are attached to the *lithah* (gums).

14. The makhraj of ظ, ذ and ث: the tip of the tongue touches the edges of the upper central incisors.[17]

Al-ḥurūf ash-shafawīyah الحُرُوْفُ الشَّفَوِيَّة

---

[16] With shīn and ṣād, some people incorrectly make their lips come together into an O-shape; in reality, the lips must remain in their default position unless their movement is specifically required or described.

[17] The tongue must not stick out (more than a few millimetres) from between the two rows of teeth, which is a common mistake with thāʾ and dhāl.

These are known as the ḥurūf shafawīyah because they are pronounced from the *shafah* (lips).

15. The makhraj of ف: the moist (inner) part of the bottom lip touches the edge of the upper central incisors.

16. The makhraj of واو مُتَحَرِّكَة, واو اللِّيْن, ب and م: these are pronounced with the lips. The differences are:

Wāw mutaḥarrikah and wāw al-līn: the lips make a rounded shape, leaving the middle open.

Bāʾ: the moist (inner) part of the lips meet.

Mīm: the dry (outer) part of the lips meet.

Ḥurūf al-ghunnah حُرُوْفُ الغُنَّة

17. The makhraj of ghunnah: the sound that comes from the *khayshūm* (nasal cavity/upper nostrils) when pronouncing the letters of ghunnah, i.e. ن and م.[18]

Note of caution

Each letter should be pronounced identically wherever it appears, e.g. if the dhāl in الَّذِيْ is pronounced properly, the same should be the case for الَّذِيْنَ, كَذَّبُوْا and تُكَذِّبَانِ.

> **Exercise:** Jot down each letter and its accompanying makhraj from memory. Don't worry if you initially make mistakes or forget; the charts and diagrams on the following three pages should help you visualise the makhārij and aid your memorisation.

[18] Nūn and mīm have a two-part makhraj: the mouth sound and the nose sound. The ghunnah, which is the nose sound, completes the makhraj of these two letters. Simply pinch your nose with your fingers whilst pronouncing them to hear what an incomplete nūn or mīm sounds like.

Makhārij summary table

حروف المدّ / الحروف الهوائية	◌َا ◌ُو ◌ِي
الحروف الحلقية	ء ه ع ح غ خ
الحروف اللهوية	ق ك
الحروف الشجرية	ج ش ي ◌َيْ
الحرف الحافي	ض
الحروف الذلقية / الحروف الطرفية	ل ن ر
الحروف النطعية	ط د ت
الحروف الأسلية / حروف الصفير	ص س ز
الحروف اللثوية	ظ ذ ث
الحروف الشفوية	ف و ◌َوْ ب م
حروف الغنّة	ن م

> **Extension task:** Draw a picture similar to the diagram on p.35, and scribble in descriptions for each makhraj, e.g. for qāf: *'the upper part of the back of the tongue touches the upper palate'*.

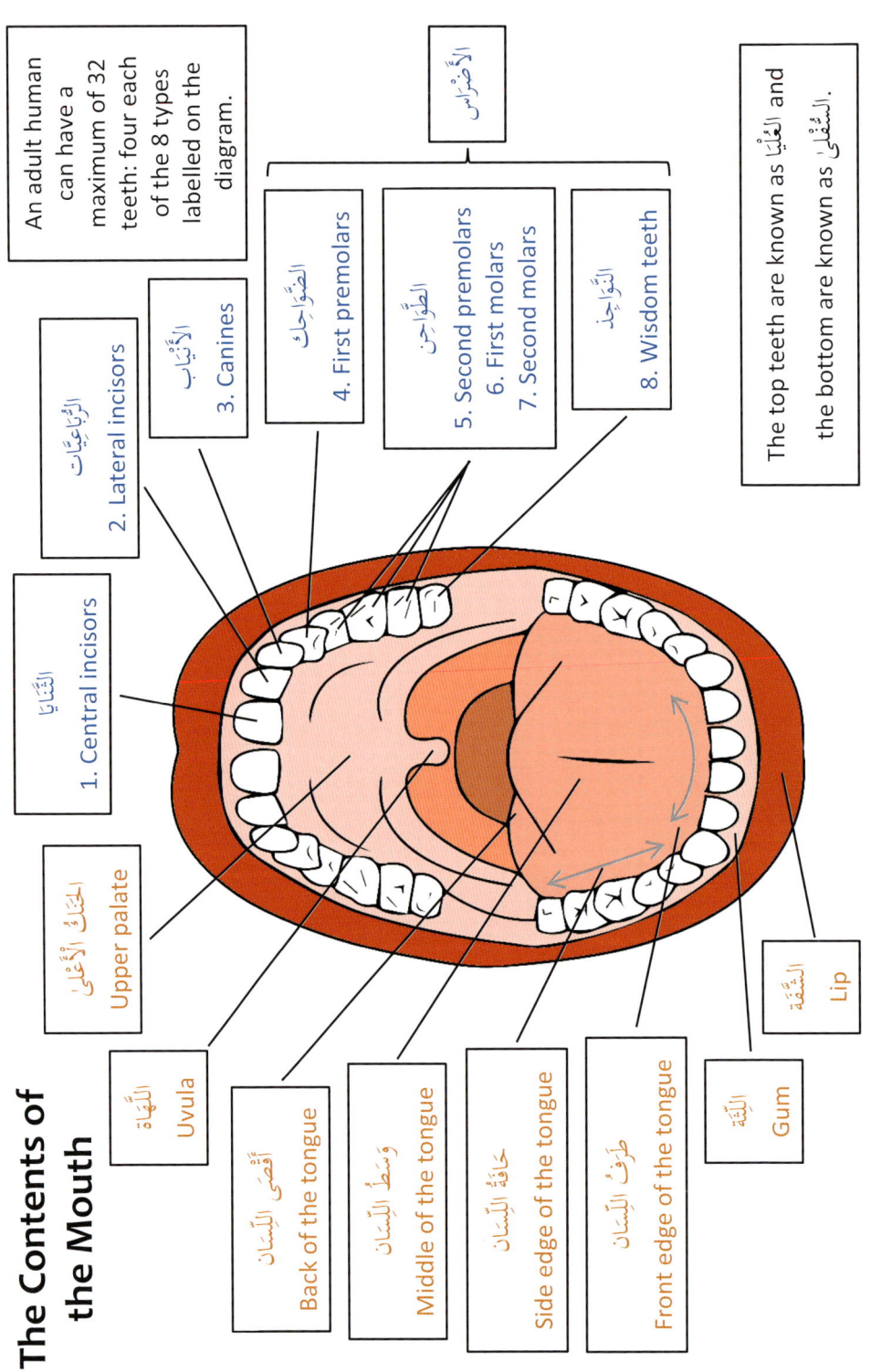

The Contents of the Mouth

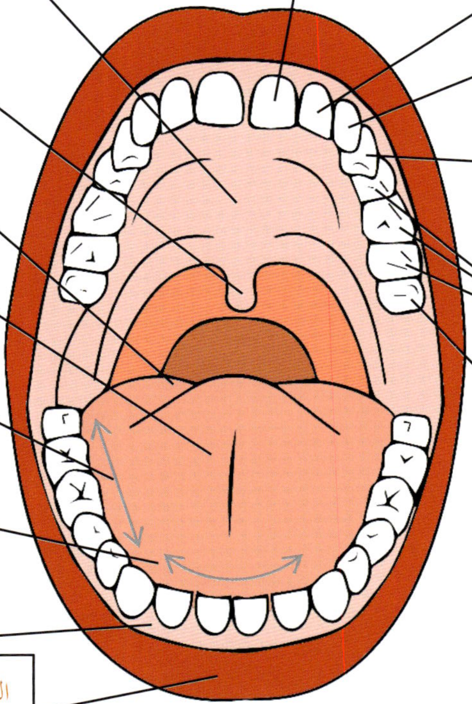

An adult human can have a maximum of 32 teeth: four each of the 8 types labelled on the diagram.

The top teeth are known as العُلْيَا and the bottom are known as السُّفْلَى.

The Places of Articulation

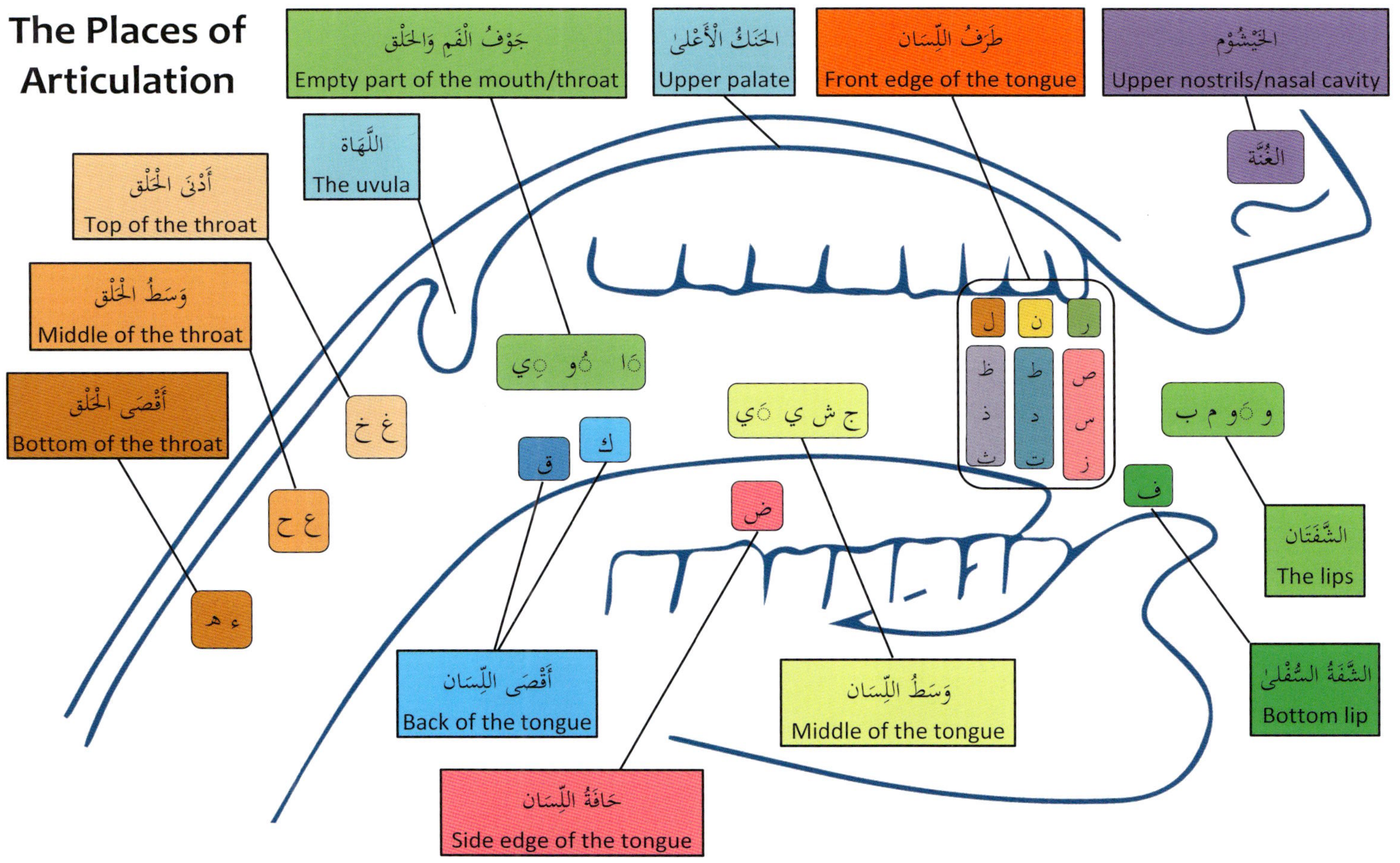

Chapter 8: Ṣifāt[19]

Literal meaning of ṣifah (plural – ṣifāt): quality, attribute, characteristic.

Technical definition: the way of pronouncing a certain letter or group of letters.

Types of ṣifāt

There are 2 types of ṣifāt:

1. **Ṣifāt lāzimah**: qualities that are always found in a letter[20]. If you neglect such a ṣifah, the letter is considered nāqiṣ (incomplete).
2. **Ṣifāt ʿāriḍah**: qualities that are sometimes found in a letter. If you neglect such a ṣifah, the beauty of the letter is lost.

Aṣ-ṣifāt al-lāzimah الصِّفَاتُ اللَّازِمَة

There are 2 types of ṣifāt lāzimah:

1. **Ṣifāt mutaḍāddah**: those ṣifāt that have opposites.
2. **Ṣifāt ghayr mutaḍāddah**: those ṣifāt that do not have opposites.

Aṣ-ṣifāt al-lāzimah al-mutaḍāddah الصِّفَاتُ اللَّازِمَةُ الْمُتَضَادَّة

There are ten ṣifāt mutaḍāddah:

1. Hams & 2. Jahr 3. Shiddah & 4. Rakhāwah 5. Istiʿlāʾ & 6. Istifāl
7. Iṭbāq & 8. Infitāḥ 9. Idhlāq & 10. Iṣmāt

1. Al-hams الهَمْس – the quiet letters

Literal meaning: to murmur, to whisper.

---

[19] Mere description of the ṣifāt is insufficient; like the makhārij, the ṣifāt cannot be understood without physical demonstration by a tajwīd specialist.

[20] All the ṣifāt lāzimah are permanently present in their respective letters in all states (except qalqalah, which is only evident in the state of sukūn), however all the ṣifāt are generally clearer when the letters are in sākin form.

There are 10 letters of hams (al-ḥurūf al-mahmūsah), which can be remembered by the following Arabic phrase: فَحَثَّهُ شَخْصٌ سَكَتْ.

When these letters are pronounced, the vocal cords stay apart; the breath remains unbroken[21] and the sound comes out low (in volume), e.g. يَلْهَثْ.

Extra care must be taken when pronouncing tāʾ and kāf, so as not to neglect the quality of hams[22].

The opposite of hams is jahr.

2. Al-jahr الجَهْر – the loud letters

Literal meaning: to be clearly audible.

Apart from the letters of hams, the rest of the 19 letters are of jahr (al-ḥurūf al-majhūrah).

When these letters are pronounced, the vocal cords come together and vibrate[23]; the breath stops and the sound comes out high (in volume, i.e. loud and clear), e.g. مَأْكُول.

3. Ash-shiddah الشِّدَّة – the hard letters

Literal meaning: forcefulness, power, strength.

There are 8 letters of shiddah (al-ḥurūf ash-shadīdah): أَجِدْ قَطٍ بَكَتْ.

---

[21] If you place your hand in front of your mouth whilst pronouncing these letters in a sākin state, you will feel the unbroken breath against your palm.
[22] This is a common mistake amongst Indo-Pak reciters.
Also, when reciting tāʾ and kāf in sākin form, make sure that the hams quality does not instead turn into a qalqalah sound.
Another common mistake (prevalent amongst Arabs) is to pronounce the tāʾ with the quality of ṣafīr (from the makhraj of sīn).
[23] If you place your fingers on your throat whilst pronouncing these letters, you will feel the vibration of the vocal cords.

When these letters are pronounced, there is hardness in the sound, and the sound stops in the makhraj[24], e.g. بِالْحَجِّ.

Please note that tāʾ and kāf are shadīdah at the beginning of their utterance and mahmūsah towards the end[25].

The opposite of shiddah is rakhāwah.

At-tawassuṭ البَيْنِيَّة / التَّوَسُّط – inbetween shiddah and rakhāwah

There are 5 letters of tawassuṭ (al-ḥurūf al-mutawassiṭah): لِنْ عُمَرْ.

When the letters of tawassuṭ are pronounced, the sound emitted is in between that of shiddah and rakhāwah, i.e. part of the sound lingers.

With lām and rāʾ, part of the sound is blocked by the tongue, and part of it continues and escapes from around the tongue.

In nūn and mīm, the sound comes out from both the nose and the mouth; the mouth sound stops, and the sound from the nose lingers.

With ʿayn, part of the sound is blocked by the epiglottis moving towards the back of the throat.

4. Ar-rakhāwah الرَّخَاوَة – the soft letters

Literal meaning: softness, looseness.

Apart from the letters of shiddah and tawassuṭ, the rest of the 16 letters are of rakhāwah (al-ḥurūf ar-rikhwah).

---

[24] In jahr and hams, it is the breath that stops or lingers, whereas in shiddah and rakhāwah, it is the sound that stops or lingers. E.g. in kāf (hams, shiddah), the breath lingers, but the sound stops; and in yāʾ (jahr, rakhāwah), the breath stops, but the sound lingers.

[25] This means that the quality of shiddah applies at the first part of pronouncing them, and hams comes at the end; whereas in thāʾ, for example, the opposite quality of rakhāwah and hams are able to coincide with each other.

When these letters are pronounced, there is softness in the sound and the sound continues beyond the makhraj, e.g. يُهْرَعُوْنَ.

5. Al-istiʿlāʾ الِاسْتِعْلَاء – the full mouth letters

Literal meaning: to rise.

There are 7 letters of istiʿlāʾ (al-ḥurūf al-mustaʿliyah): خُصَّ ضَغْطٍ قِظْ.

When these letters are pronounced, most of the root of the tongue rises towards the upper palate, and the letters are pronounced with a full mouth, e.g. أَخْرِجُوْهُمْ.

The opposite of istiʿlāʾ is istifāl.

6. Al-istifāl الِاسْتِفَال – the empty mouth letters

Literal meaning: to descend.

Apart from the letters of istiʿlāʾ, the rest of the 22 letters are of istifāl (al-ḥurūf al-mustafilah).

When these letters are pronounced, most of the root of the tongue does not rise towards the upper palate, and the letters are pronounced with an empty mouth, e.g. the dhāl of يَذْهَبُوْا.

7. Al-iṭbāq الإِطْبَاق – the closed letters

Literal meaning: to join.

There are 4 letters of iṭbāq (al-ḥurūf al-muṭbaqah): ص ض ط ظ.

When these letters are pronounced, much of the tongue meets with the upper palate, and the sound is confined between the tongue and upper palate, e.g. the ṭāʾ of مَطْلَعِ.

The opposite of iṭbāq is infitāḥ.

8. Al-infitāḥ الاِنْفِتَاح – the open letters

Literal meaning: to separate.

Apart from the letters of iṭbāq, the rest of the 25 letters are of infitāḥ (al-ḥurūf al-munfatiḥah).

When these letters are pronounced, the tongue remains sufficiently separated from the upper palate, allowing the sound to escape from the interior of the mouth, e.g. يَنْحِتُوْنَ.

9. Al-idhlāq الإِذْلَاق – the edge letters

Literal meaning: to sharpen.

There are 6 letters of idhlāq (al-ḥurūf al-mudhlaqah): فَرَّ مِنْ لُّبِّ.

These letters are pronounced from the edge of the tongue or lips; lām, nūn and rā' are pronounced from the dhalq al-lisān (tip of the tongue), whereas fā', bā' and mīm are pronounced from the dhalq ash-shafah (edge of the lips).

The opposite of idhlāq is iṣmāt.

10. Al-iṣmāt الإِصْمَات – the prevented letters

Literal meaning: to prevent.

Apart from the letters of idhlāq, the rest of the 23 letters are of iṣmāt (al-ḥurūf al-muṣmatah).

This quality and its opposite ṣifah are not connected with the rules of pronunciation, but are used to differentiate between original Arabic roots and foreign loan-words in ṣarf (Arabic morphology)[26]; these letters

---

[26] Imām Ibn al-Jazarī ﷺ included idhlāq and iṣmāt in the ṣifāt, because when they were first defined, tajwīd and ṣarf had not yet separated into two distinct disciplines.

are *prevented* from exclusively appearing in rubāʿī or khumāsī root words without the presence of a ḥarf mudhlaq[27].

Aṣ-ṣifāt al-lāzimah ghayr al-mutaḍāddah الصِّفَاتُ اللَّازِمَةُ غَيْرُ الْمُتَضَادَّة

There are seven ṣifāt ghayr mutaḍāddah: 1) ṣafīr, 2) qalqalah, 3) līn, 4) inḥirāf, 5) takrīr, 6) tafashshi, and 7) istiṭālah.

1. Aṣ-ṣafīr الصَّفِيْر

Literal meaning: to whistle, to hiss.

There are 3 letters of ṣafīr (ḥurūf aṣ-ṣafīr): ص س ز.

These letters are pronounced sharply, like a whistle[28], e.g. أَصْغَرَ.

2. Al-qalqalah القَلْقَلَة

Literal meaning: to shake, to move.

There are 5 letters of qalqalah (al-ḥurūf al-muqalqalah): قُطْبُ جَدٍ.

These letters are pronounced with vibration/movement (i.e. an echoing sound[29]) when they are in the state of sākin, e.g. خَلَق.

There are three types of qalqalah: ṣughrā (weak), kubrā (strong) and aqwā (strongest):

---

[27] If there are no ḥurūf mudhlaqah in a rubāʿī or khumāsī root word, then that word is not Arabic in origin.

[28] The sharpness in the sound occurs because it must pass through a very narrow space, i.e. between the teeth, similar to the act of whistling. The strength of this sharpness is evident when a person is reciting quietly (e.g. in ṣalāh): the listener will always hear the hiss of the ṣād, sīn or zāʾ, if nothing else.

[29] Care must be taken that such echoing sounds do not go to the extent of forming any ḥarakāh or tashdīd; in qalqalah, the lips move apart, but the jaws do not, whereas in pronouncing a ḥarakāh, the lips and jaws will both move.

1. Ṣughrā: qalqalah during waṣl, e.g. in أَدْرَاكَ and قَدْ أَفْلَحَ. The echo sound is not as strong.

2. Kubrā: qalqalah at the end of a word during waqf, e.g. in كُفُوًا أَحَد. The echo sound is stronger.

3. Aqwā[30]: qalqalah at the end of a word during waqf, when the muqalqal letter also has a shaddah on it, e.g in وَتَبّ. The echo sound is at its strongest, to indicate towards the presence of tashdīd.

3. Al-līn اللِّيْن

Literal meaning: to be soft.

There are 2 letters of līn (ḥurūf al-līn): و and ي. The quality of līn is found in them when they are sākin and the letter before them is maftūḥ.

These letters are pronounced softly (with ease), and they are stretched in a similar way to the ḥurūf al-madd, e.g. خَوْفٌ and بَيْتٌ.

Care must be taken not to over-pronounce these letters, i.e. with force and heaviness.

4. Al-inḥirāf الإِنْحِرَاف

Literal meaning: to turn, to deviate.

There are 2 letters of inḥirāf (al-ḥurūf al-munḥarifah): ل and ر.

When these letters are pronounced, the sound moves away from its original path due to the tongue blocking its way, e.g. قُلْ and فَارْغَبْ.

---

[30] According to some scholars, this qalqalah strength does not exist, as they do not recognise the need to differentiate a mushaddad letter from a non-mushaddad letter during waqf.

When pronouncing the lām, the sound exits around both sides of the ṭaraf al-lisān, as it is blocked by the tip.

When pronouncing the rāʾ, the sound moves back from the sides of the ṭaraf al-lisān, and exits through a slight opening created in the middle of the ṭaraf al-lisān.

5. At-takrīr التَّكْرِيْر

Literal meaning: to repeat.

This quality is found in the letter ر (also known as al-ḥarf al-mukarrar).

When this letter is pronounced, particularly in sākin or mushaddad form, there will be a vibration in the tongue. However, this vibration must *not* be exaggerated to create multiple rāʾ sounds, as repetition or trilling must be avoided.[31]

6. At-tafashshi التَّفَشِّي

Literal meaning: to spread out.

This quality is found in the letter ش (also known as al-ḥarf al-mutafashshi).

When this letter is pronounced, the sound spreads throughout the mouth, e.g. يَشْكُرُوْنَ.

7. Al-istiṭālah الاِسْتِطَالَة

Literal meaning: to stretch out, to become long.

This quality is found in the letter ض (also known as al-ḥarf al-mustaṭīl).

[31] This quality is mentioned so that the reciter can minimise it, rather than actively implement it. When pronounced correctly, the 'rolling' of the rāʾ will be very slight, but not completely eliminated.

When this letter is pronounced, the sound is stretched out across its whole makhraj, from beginning to end, i.e. all along the ḥāfat al-lisān (upturned sides of the tongue), e.g. يَضْرِب.

The tongue hits the roots of the top molars from back to front[32] in quick succession, until the front of the tongue reaches the roots of the upper incisors; the sound is slightly prolonged[33] as a result. Thus, ḍād is not a ḥarf shadīd like the dāl.

Aṣ-ṣifāt al-ʿāriḍah الصِّفَاتُ الْعَارِضَة

When a quality is sometimes found in a letter, and sometimes not, then this is known as a ṣifah ʿāriḍah, e.g. the rules of tafkhīm, tarqīq, idghām, ikhfāʾ, madd, etc.

Exercise: Use the chart on p.46 to demonstrate the ṣifāt, letter by letter. Only move on to the next letter once you have understood all the ṣifāt of the current letter and how to apply them in practice.

Extension task: Go through *Bāb Ṣifāt al-Ḥurūf* from the Jazarīyah Poem, along with its English translation (see *Appendix 2*). You could sing along and memorise it with Saʿd al-Ghāmidī's rendition of the poem, which is widely available on YouTube. Reciting/memorising this section will help you easily recall all the ṣifāt and their associated letters.

[32] Or front to back, if that is easier.

[33] The sound of a ḍād sākinah is prolonged for a duration slightly less than one alif.

Ṣifāt Summary Diagrams

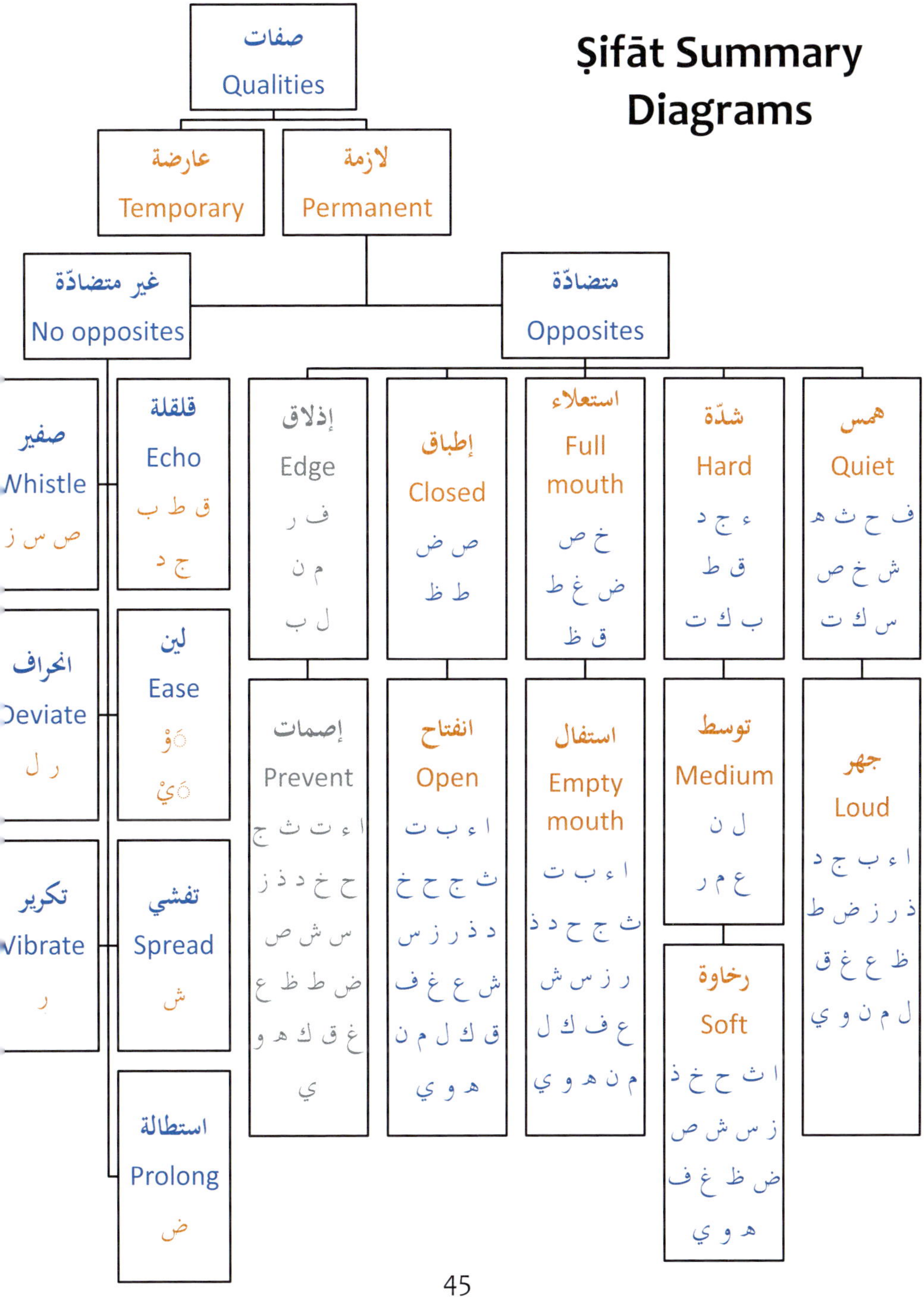

صفات
Qualities
عارضة
Temporary
لازمة
Permanent
غير متضادّة
No opposites
متضادّة
Opposites
همس
Quiet
ف ح ث ه
ش خ ص
س ك ت
شدّة
Hard
ء ج د
ق ط
ب ك ت
استعلاء
Full mouth
خ ص
ض غ ط
ق ظ
إطباق
Closed
ص ض
ط ظ
إذلاق
Edge
ف ر
م ن
ل ب
جهر
Loud
ا ء ب ج د
ذ ر ز ض ط
ظ ع غ ق
ل م ن و ي
توسط
Medium
ل ن
ع م ر
رخاوة
Soft
ا ث ح خ ذ
ز س ش ص
ض ظ غ ف
ه و ي
استفال
Empty mouth
ا ء ب ت
ث ج ح د ذ
ر ز س ش
ع ف ك ل
م ن ه و ي
انفتاح
Open
ا ء ب ت
ث ج ح خ
د ذ ر ز س
ش ع غ ف
ق ك ل م ن
ه و ي
إصمات
Prevent
ا ء ت ث ج
ح خ د ذ ز
س ش ص
ض ط ظ ع
غ ق ك ه و
ي
قلقلة
Echo
ق ط ب
ج د
لين
Ease
ـَوْ
ـَيْ
تفشي
Spread
ش
استطالة
Prolong
ض
صفير
histle
ص س ز
انحراف
eviate
ل ر
تكرير
ibrate
ر

ا: جهر، رخاوة، استفال، انفتاح، إصمات	ء: جهر، شدّة، استفال، انفتاح، إصمات	ب: جهر، شدّة، استفال، انفتاح، إذلاق، قلقلة	ت: همس، شدّة، استفال، انفتاح، إصمات
ث: همس، رخاوة، استفال، انفتاح، إصمات	ج: جهر، شدّة، استفال، انفتاح، إصمات، قلقلة	ح: همس، رخاوة، استفال، انفتاح، إصمات	خ: همس، رخاوة، استعلاء، انفتاح، إصمات
د: جهر، شدّة، استفال، انفتاح، إصمات، قلقلة	ذ: جهر، رخاوة، استفال، انفتاح، إصمات	ر: جهر، توسط، استفال، انفتاح، إذلاق، انحراف، تكرير	ز: جهر، رخاوة، استفال، انفتاح، إصمات، صفير
س: همس، رخاوة، استفال، انفتاح، إصمات، صفير	ش: همس، رخاوة، استفال، انفتاح، إصمات، تفشي	ص: همس، رخاوة، استعلاء، إطباق، إصمات، صفير	ض: جهر، رخاوة، استعلاء، إطباق، إصمات، استطالة
ط: جهر، شدّة، استعلاء، إطباق، إصمات، قلقلة	ظ: جهر، رخاوة، استعلاء، إطباق، إصمات	ع: جهر، توسط، استفال، انفتاح، إصمات	غ: جهر، رخاوة، استعلاء، انفتاح، إصمات
ف: همس، رخاوة، استفال، انفتاح، إذلاق	ق: جهر، شدّة، استعلاء، انفتاح، إصمات، قلقلة	ك: همس، شدّة، استفال، انفتاح، إصمات	ل: جهر، توسط، استفال، انفتاح، إذلاق، انحراف
م: جهر، توسط، استفال، انفتاح، إذلاق	ن: جهر، توسط، استفال، انفتاح، إذلاق	هـ: همس، رخاوة، استفال، انفتاح، إصمات	و: جهر، رخاوة، استفال، انفتاح، إصمات، لين
ي: جهر، رخاوة، استفال، انفتاح، إصمات، لين			

Chapter 9: Ḥarakāt and sukūn

Al-ḥarakāt الحَرَكَات

There are 3 ḥarakāt (short vowel signs):

ḍammah (ـُ)   fatḥah (ـَ)   kasrah (ـِ)

A letter with a ḥarakah on it is called mutaḥarrik (مُتَحَرِّك).

When reading the Qur᾿ān, these 3 ḥarakāt should be pronounced in a maʿrūf (active) way, and not a majhūl (passive) way.

1. Aḍ-ḍammat al-maʿrūfah الضَّمَّةُ الْمَعْرُوْفَة

To emit a sound whilst making a closed O-shape with the lips.

A letter with a ḍammah on it is called maḍmūm (مَضْمُوْم).

2. Al-fatḥat al-maʿrūfah الفَتْحَةُ الْمَعْرُوْفَة

To emit a sound whilst the mouth is open; the shape of the lips remains flat and not rounded like when making a ḍammah sound.

A letter with a fatḥah on it is called maftūḥ (مَفْتُوْح).

3. Al-kasrat al-maʿrūfah الكَسْرَةُ الْمَعْرُوْفَة

To emit a sound whilst the mouth is inclined; the lower jaw drops slightly and the middle of the tongue rises upwards.

A letter with a kasrah on it is called maksūr (مَكْسُوْر).

Ḍammah maqlūbah (ٗ◌), **fatḥah qāʾimah** (ٰ◌) and **kasrah qāʾimah** (ٖ◌) are treated the same as the ḥurūf al-madd[34], and must be stretched for the duration of one alif[35]. If they are not stretched, they become nāqiṣ (incomplete).

As-sukūn السُّكُوْن

Sukūn means: (verb) to read a letter without a ḥarakah on it, (noun) non-vowel sign (ْ◌). A letter with a sukūn on it is known as sākin (سَاكِن).

The sukūn must be pronounced properly, so that not even a little bit of ḥarakah sound is emitted. In order to do this, the sound of the sākin letter will stop in its makhraj, and the next letter will immediately be pronounced.

When tāʾ and kāf are read in waqf (as sākin), they are pronounced softly, so that the naturally occurring sound of qalqalah becomes absolutely minimal.

Ash-shaddah الشَّدَّة

When a letter is repeated twice in a word and there is no ḥarakah on the first one, the letter is written once and a shaddah (ّ◌) is placed on top of it, e.g.

رَ بْ بِ = رَبِّ

A letter with a shaddah on it is known as mushaddad (مُشَدَّد).

---

[34] Ḍammah maqlūbah is considered equivalent to wāw maddīyah, fatḥah muqaddarah (آ) and fatḥah qāʾimah are equivalent to alif maddīyah, and kasrah qāʾimah is equivalent to yāʾ maddīyah.

[35] The duration of one alif can be determined by the normal opening or closing of a finger. It is equivalent to two 'counts' or ḥarakāt (an alternative measurement used in some tajwīd books and courses).

Nūn mushaddadah and mīm mushaddadah

If a shaddah appears on a nūn or mīm, they will be recited with ghunnah, for the duration of one alif, e.g.

إِنَّ   ثُمَّ

This ghunnah will also take place in waqf, e.g.

فِيْهِنّ   جَانّ

Al-ḥarakat al-ʿariḍīyah الحَرَكَةُ العَارِضِيَّة

A temporary ḥarakah given to a letter that is originally sākin. This usually happens if the letter is joined to the word after, or recited separately from the word before, e.g.

إِذْ ← وَإِذِ ابْتَلٰى   قُلْنَا ادْخُلُوا ← أُدْخُلوا

> **Exercise:** Make a summary table of the symbols and their corresponding Arabic names, along with any other names you may know them by.

Chapter 10: Tafkhīm and tarqīq

At-tafkhīm التَّفْخِيم

To pronounce a letter with a full mouth, e.g.

خَا   صَا   ضَا

A letter pronounced with tafkhīm is known as mufakhkham (مُفَخَّم).

The 7 ḥurūf mustaʿliyah (خُصَّ ضَغْطٍ قِظْ) are always full mouth letters.

When pronouncing a letter with tafkhīm, it must not be overdone:

1) If a mufakhkham letter is maksūr, it must not sound as if there is a fatḥah on it.

2) If a mufakhkham letter has a fatḥah on it, it must not sound like a maḍmūm[36].

3) If a mufakhkham letter has an alif after it, the alif must not sound like a wāw.

Stages of tafkhīm

There are 4 stages of tafkhīm, according to how strong the full mouth quality manifests within the mufakhkham letter.

The list below goes from strongest to weakest:

1. When the full mouth letter is maftūḥ, and has an alif after it, e.g. الطَّالِبُ
2. When the full mouth letter is maftūḥ, with no alif after it, e.g. اِنْطَلِقُوْا
3. When the full mouth letter is maḍmūm, e.g. طُبِعَ
4. When the full mouth letter is maksūr, e.g. طِبَاقًا

---

[36] Extra care must be taken so that the shape of the lips remains flat.

The strength of a mufakhkham letter that is sākin will be determined by the ḥarakah of the letter before it[37]:

- The khā' sākin in تَخْتَلِفُوْنَ has a stage 2 tafkhīm strength.
- The khā' sākin in مُخْتَلِفٍ has a stage 3 tafkhīm strength.
- The khā' sākin in اِخْتِلَافًا has a stage 4 tafkhīm strength.

At-tarqīq التَّرْقِيْق

To pronounce a letter with an empty mouth, e.g.

مَا كَا بَا

A letter pronounced with tarqīq is known as muraqqaq (مُرَقَّق).

The ḥurūf mustafilah are always pronounced with an empty mouth, except for alif maddīyah, the lām in الله and rā'. These letters are sometimes pronounced with tafkhīm, and sometimes with tarqīq.

When pronouncing a letter with tarqīq, it must not be overdone so that it sounds like imālāh sughrā (see *Chapter 19*), e.g. the وٰى in the word تَقْوٰى is pronounced as 'taq-wā', not 'taq-wear'.

The rule of alif maddīyah

1) If there is a full mouth letter before an alif, then the alif will also be pronounced with tafkhīm, e.g.

قَال طَال

2) If there is an empty mouth letter before an alif, the alif will also be pronounced with tarqīq, e.g.

---

[37] According to some scholars, a full-mouth letter that is a sākin has its own tafkhim strength, above the 4th stage mentioned.

مَالَ   سَالَتْ

The ruling of alif is neither tafkhīm nor tarqīq; it follows the ruling of the letter before it.

The rule of the lām in the word الله

1) If there is a fatḥah or ḍammah before the lām in the word الله, then it will be pronounced with tafkhīm, e.g.

خَتَمَ اللّٰهُ   سُبْحٰنَكَ اللّٰهُمَّ   نَصَرَكُمُ اللّٰهُ

2) If there is a kasrah before it, then the lām in the word الله will be pronounced with tarqīq, e.g.

بِسْمِ اللّٰهِ   مِنْ عِنْدِ اللّٰهِ   وَمَنْ يَّعْصِ اللّٰهَ

Note of caution

It is very important to pronounce muraqqaq letters properly, without the slightest bit of tafkhīm.

If a mufakhkham letter comes near a bāʾ or lām, take care in pronouncing the bāʾ or lām with tarqīq, e.g. in the following words:

بِالْبٰطِلِ   بَغْيٌ   بَرْقٌ   وَلْيَتَلَطَّفْ   وَلَا الضَّآلِّيْنَ

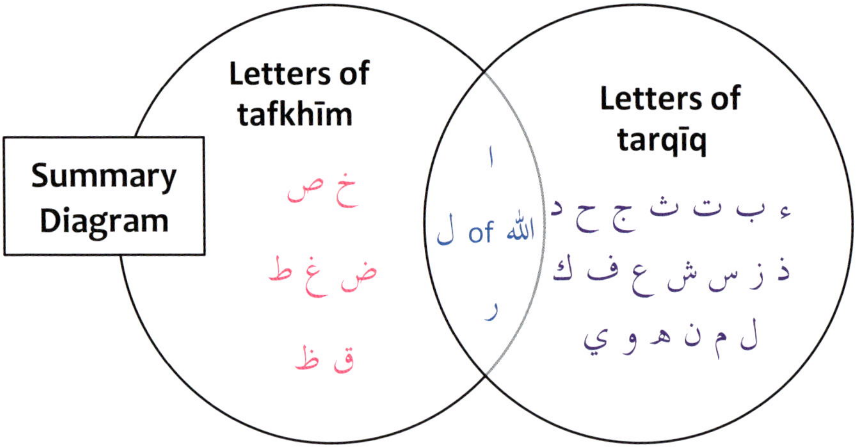

Chapter 11: Rules of the letter rāʾ

The letter rāʾ appears in 3 states:

1. Rāʾ mutaḥarrikah
2. Rāʾ sākinah mā qablahā mutaḥarrik (rāʾ sākinah with a mutaḥarrik before it)
3. Rāʾ sākinah [mā qablahā] sākin mā qablahū mutaḥarrik (rāʾ sākinah with a sākin before it, and a mutaḥarrik before that)

Ar-rāʾ al-mutaḥarrikah الرَّاءُ الْمُتَحَرِّكَة

1) If there is a fatḥah or ḍammah on a rāʾ, it will be read with tafkhīm, e.g.

رُزِقْنَا   رَبَّنَا

2) If there is a kasrah under a rāʾ, it will be read with tarqīq, e.g.

رِجَالًا   رِزْقًا

Ar-rāʾ as-sākinah mā qablahā mutaḥarrik الرَّاءُ السَّاكِنَة مَا قَبْلَهَا مُتَحَرِّك

1) If there is a fatḥah or ḍammah before a rāʾ sākinah, then the rāʾ sākinah will be read with tafkhīm, e.g.

يُرْزَقُونَ   يَرْجِعُونَ

There are three exceptions to the above:

يَسْرِ (سورة الفجر)   أَسْرِ (سورة طٰه)   نُذُرِ (سورة القمر)

In waqf, it is better to recite these with tarqīq, to indicate towards the 'hidden' yāʾ (after the rāʾ) in these words.

2) If there is a kasrah before a rāʾ sākinah, then the rāʾ sākinah will be read with tarqīq, as long as 3 criteria are met:

a) The kasrah before the rāʾ sākinah must be aṣlīyah (original), e.g.

أَنْذِرْهُمْ بِشِرْكِكُمْ

If the kasrah is ʿāriḍīyah (temporary) and not aṣlīyah, then the rāʾ will be read with tafkhīm, e.g.

اِرْجِعُوْا أَمِ ارْتَابُوْا

b) The kasrah before the rāʾ sākinah must be in the same word, e.g.

أَنْذِرْهُمْ يَغْفِرْلَكُمْ

If the kasrah is in another word, then the rāʾ will be read with tafkhīm, e.g.

رَبِّ ارْجِعُوْنِ أَمِ ارْتَابُوْا

c) After the rāʾ sākinah, there is no ḥarf mustaʿlī[38] in the same word, e.g.

أَنْذِرْهُمْ

If after the rāʾ sākinah, there is a ḥarf mustaʿlī in the same word, then the rāʾ will be pronounced with tafkhīm, e.g. [39]

فِرْقَةٌ إِرْصَادًا قِرْطَاسٍ مِرْصَادًا

If the ḥarf mustaʿlī is in the next word, then the rāʾ will be pronounced with tarqīq, e.g.

وَلَا تُصَعِّرْ خَدَّكَ فَاصْبِرْ صَبْرًا

---

[38] مُسْتَعْلٍ – singular form of the word ‘mustaʿliyah’.

[39] These are the only examples to be found in the Qur’ān.

Exception: in the word فِرْقٍ, you can pronounce the rā' with tafkhīm or tarqīq [40].

Ar-rā' as-sākinah [mā qablahā] sākin mā qablahū mutaḥarrik الرَّاء السَّاكِنَة (مَا قَبْلَهَا) سَاكِن مَا قَبْلَه مُتَحَرِّك

Please note that this rule applies when making waqf, i.e. when the rā' is mawqūfah (sākin due to stopping).

1) If the letter before a rā' sākinah has a sukūn on it, and the letter before that has a fatḥah or ḍammah on it, then the rā' will be read with tafkhīm, e.g.

قَدْرْ أُمُوْرْ

2) If the letter before a rā' sākinah has a sukūn on it, and the letter before that has a kasrah under it, then the rā' will be read with tarqīq, e.g.

ذِكْرْ حِجْرْ

3) However, if the letter before the rā' sākinah is a yā' sākinah, then the rā' will be read with tarqīq in every situation, e.g.

ضَيْرْ خَيْرْ نَذِيْرْ

Ar-rā' al-mushaddadah الرَّاءُ الْمُشَدَّدَة

The rule for rā' mushaddadah is the same as the rule for one rā':

1) If the rā' mushaddadah has a fatḥah or ḍammah on it, then it will be read with tafkhīm, e.g.

---

[40] The qurrā' who recited it with tarqīq took into consideration the kasrahs on either side of the rā, whilst the qurrā' who recited it with tafkhīm took into consideration the letter of isti'lā' after the rā' sākinah.

وَالرُّوحُ

يَعْلَمُ السِّرَّ

2) If the rā' mushaddadah has a kasrah under it, then it will be read with tarqīq, e.g.

دُرِّيٌّ

3) If the rā' mushaddadah is sākin, and the letter before it has a fatḥah or ḍammah on it, then the rā' mushaddadah will be read with tafkhīm, e.g.

لَا يَضُرّ ○   مُسْتَقَرّ ○

4) If the rā' mushaddadah is sākin, and the letter before it has a kasrah under it, then the rā' mushaddadah will be read with tarqīq, e.g.

مُسْتَمِرّ ○

Ar-rā' al-mumālah الرَّاءُ الْمُمَالَة

The rā' mumālah (that upon which imālah is carried out) will be recited with tarqīq. This only takes place in verse 41 of Sūrat Hūd:

بِسْمِ اللهِ مَجْرٖىهَا وَمُرْسٰىهَا

Ar-rā' al-murāmah الرَّاءُ الْمُرَامَة

Rawm is a light sound that can only be carried out on a letter that has a ḍammah or kasrah on it. In rawm, one third of the ḥarakah is pronounced and two thirds of it is left out (see *Chapter 21*).

Rule for the rā' murāmah (that upon which rawm is carried out) [41]:

---

[41] حُكْمُهُ حُكْمُ الْوَصْل – the rule of a murāmah letter is that of waṣl, i.e. the way it is pronounced in the state of waṣl, the same rulings apply in the state of waqf bi 'r-rawm.

1) If waqf bi ‘r-rawm is carried out on a rāʾ that has a ḍammah on it, then the rāʾ will be pronounced with tafkhīm, e.g.

وَإِلَيْكَ الْمَصِيْرُ   عَلَىٰ كُلِّ شَيْءٍ قَدِيْرٌ

2) If waqf bi ‘r-rawm is carried out on a rāʾ that has kasrah under it, then the rāʾ will be pronounced with tarqīq, e.g.

عَذَابَ النَّارِ   غَيْرَ تَخْسِيْرٍ

The rāʾ of miṣr and qiṭr

When waqf is carried out on the word مِصْر it is better to read the rāʾ with tafkhīm, because in the state of waṣl that rāʾ would be read with tafkhīm, i.e.

أَلَيْسَ لِيْ مُلْكُ مِصْرَ

When waqf is carried out on the word قِطْر it is better to read the rāʾ with tarqīq, because in the state of waṣl that rāʾ would be read with tarqīq, i.e.

وَأَسَلْنَا لَهُ عَيْنَ الْقِطْرِ

Exercise: Look into the Qurʾān and pick out 15 words that contain the letter rāʾ. Use two different colours of highlighter to show whether they will be recited with tafkhīm or tarqīq.

Extension task: Draw a mind map of all the rāʾ rules, making sure to use the rule name, rule number and one example of each rule. Glancing at any branch should jog your memory and bring the full rule to mind.

Chapter 12: Idghām

Al-idghām الإِدْغَام

1. To combine one letter with another and recite with tashdīd.
2. To combine two letters that are mutamāthilayn, mutajānisayn or mutaqāribayn in such a way that they become like one ḥarf mushaddad, and are pronounced making only one sound.

The letter upon which idghām is carried out (the sākin letter) is called mudgham, and the letter in which the mudgham is combined (the mutaḥarrik letter) is called mudgham fīh.

In terms of cause (or according to the ḥarf), there are 3 types of idghām:

1. **Al-mutamāthilayn** المُتَمَاثِلَيْن/المِثْلَيْن: when both letters are the same, e.g.

   إِذْ ذَّهَبَ　　　　قَدْ دَّخَلُوْا

2. **Al-mutajānisayn** المُتَجَانِسَيْن: when both letters have the same makhraj (place of origin), e.g.

   قَدْ تَّبَيَّنَ　　　　إِذْ ظَّلَمُوْا

3. **Al-mutaqāribayn** المُتَقَارِبَيْن: when both letters are close in terms of makhārij and/or ṣifāt, e.g.

   قُلْ رَّبِّ　　　　أَلَمْ نَخْلُقْكُّمْ

Note: When two letters are different in terms of makhārij and ṣifāt, they are known as *mutabā'idayn*, e.g. فَرَضْتُمْ. There is no idghām in such cases.

In terms of state, there are 2 types of idghām:

1. **Al-idghām at-tāmm** الإِدْغَامُ التَّامّ: when the qualities of the mudgham do not remain, e.g.

صَرْحًا لَّعَلِّى

In this example, the mudgham is the nūn in the tanwīn (صَرْحَنْ لَّعَلِّيْ).

2. **Al-idghām an-nāqiṣ الإِدْغَامُ النَّاقِص**: when any of the qualities of the mudgham remain, e.g.

مَنْ يَّقُوْلُ

In this example, the nasal quality of the nūn remains.

- In idghām mutamāthilayn, idghām tāmm is the rule.
- In idghām mutajānisayn, idghām tāmm will generally occur, e.g.

يَلْهَثْ ذّٰلِكَ   ارْكَبْ مَّعَنَا   إِنْ كِدْتَّ   إِذْ ظَّلَمْتُمْ

أُجِيْبَتْ دَّعْوَتُكُمَا   وَدَّتْ طَّآئِفَةٌ

However, idghām nāqiṣ will occur when the mudgham is a stronger letter than the mudgham fīh, as in the following exceptions:

لَئِنْ بَسَطْتَّ   مَافَرَّطْتُّمْ   أَحَطْتُّ   مَافَرَّطْتُ

Here, the qualities of istiʿlāʾ and iṭbāq will remain in the ṭāʾ sākinah, but the ṣifah qalqalah will be left out (qalqalah does not occur on a ḥarf mudgham).

- In idghām mutaqāribayn, both idghām tāmm and idghām nāqiṣ occur.
- In أَلَمْ نَخْلُقْكُّمْ, idghām tāmm (not to pronounce the qāf at all) is better. However, idghām nāqiṣ (when the quality of istiʿlāʾ in the qāf remains, but qalqalah is left out) is also permitted.[42]

[42] This is the only place where idghām nāqiṣ may occur in idghām mutaqāribayn, according to the riwāyah of Imām Ḥafs ﷺ.

Chapter 13: Iẓhār and idghām in alif lām at-taʿrīf

If any of the 14 letters in إِبْغِ حَجَّكَ وَخَفْ عَقِيْمَهُ appear after an alif lām at-taʿrīf (ال), the lām at-taʿrīf will be read with iẓhār (the lām will be pronounced clearly), e.g.

الْأَوَّلُ الْبَاسِطُ الْغَفُوْرُ الْحَكِيْمُ الْجَلِيْلُ

الْكَرِيْمُ الْوَدُوْدُ الْخَبِيْرُ الْفَائِزُ

الْعَلِيْمُ الْقَمَرُ الْيَقِيْنُ الْمَلِكُ الْهُدٰى

These letters are called al-ḥurūf al-qamarīyah.

Apart from the 14 ḥurūf qamarīyah, if any of the rest of the letters appear after a lām at-taʿrīf, idghām will be carried out on the lām at-taʿrīf (it will be incorporated into the next letter), e.g.

الطَّيِّبٰتُ الثَّوَابُ الصَّلٰوةُ الرَّحْمٰنُ التَّوَّابُ

الضَّأْنُ الدَّاعِ الذّٰرِيٰتُ النَّاسُ

السَّمَاءُ الظّٰهِرَةُ الزَّيْتُوْنُ الشَّيْءُ اللَّطِيْفُ

These letters are known as al-ḥurūf ash-shamsīyah.

Exercise: Jot down the 'letters of the moon' and the 'letters of the sun' in a summary table, along with some other examples from the Qurʾān.

Chapter 14: Rules of mīm sākinah

Al-mīm as-sākinah الْمِيْمُ السَّاكِنَة

Mīm sākinah is when there is a sukūn on the mīm. It appears in 3 states:

1. Idghām
2. Ikhfā᾿
3. Iẓhār

Idghām al-mīm as-sākinah إِدْغَامُ الْمِيْمِ السَّاكِنَة

If after a mīm sākinah, another mīm appears, then both mīms will be combined, and recited with ghunnah, e.g.

فِيْ قُلُوْبِهِمْ مَّرَضٌ

This idghām is known as idghām shafawī.

Ikhfā᾿ al-mīm as-sākinah إِخْفَاءُ الْمِيْمِ السَّاكِنَة

If after a mīm sākinah, a bā᾿ appears, ikhfā᾿ will be performed on the mīm sākinah; the sound of the mīm will remain completely, and it will be recited with ghunnah, e.g.

تَرْمِيْهِمْ بِحِجَارَةٍ

This ikhfā᾿ is known as ikhfā᾿ shafawī[43].

---

[43] Some reciters pronounce the ikhfā᾿ shafawī similar to the ikhfā᾿ of the nūn, i.e. by 'hiding' the mīm – our position is that the correct method is to fully pronounce the mīm with ghunnah.

The rationale behind the name ikhfā᾿ in this case is that reciting mīm with ghunnah is neither iẓhār (as ghunnah cannot occur in iẓhār), nor is it idghām (as the mīm is not incorporated into the bā᾿) - thus it is *a sound between iẓhār and idghām*, which is the exact definition of ikhfā᾿.

Also, as explained by Shaykh Ayman Suwayd, the rules of idghām etc. generally came about to create ease in pronunciation, however pronouncing ikhfā᾿ shafawī like the

Iẓhār al-mīm as-sākinah إِظْهَارُ المِيْمِ السَّاكِنَة

If after a mīm sākinah, any of the remaining 26 letters (apart from mīm, bā and alif) appear, then the mīm sākinah will be read with iẓhār; ghunnah will not be made, e.g.

أَلَمْ تَرَ   عَلَيْهِمْ وَلَا الضَّآلِّيْنَ

This iẓhār is known as iẓhār shafawī.

Note of caution

If a fā᾽ or wāw appears after a mīm sākinah, care must be taken to pronounce the mīm sākinah properly, with full iẓhār. Idghām or ikhfā᾽ shafawī must be avoided, e.g.

أَنَّهُمْ فِيْ كُلِّ   أَشْيَاءَهُمْ وَلَاتَعْثَوْا

Exercise: Choose a page of the Qur᾽ān at random, and identify within it all the iẓhār, idghām, ikhfā᾽ and qalb rules mentioned in Chapters 12, 14 & 15. Specify the exact type of each rule, e.g ikhfā᾽ *ḥaqīqī,* iẓhār *shafawī,* idghām *nāqiṣ.*

Extension task: Make revision notes for all the rules covered in Chapters 12, 14 & 15, using tables, charts or diagrams that will aid your memorisation. Be sure to include coloured examples.

---

ikhfā᾽ of the nūn goes against this principle. E.g. the word عَنْبَر is naturally pronounced as عَمْبَر for ease. Therefore, to forcibly pronounce the mīm as a nūn in recitation is unnatural and hard for the reciter.

Chapter 15: Rules of nūn sākinah and tanwīn

An-nūn as-sākinah النُّوْنُ السَّاكِنَة

Nūn sākinah is a nūn that has no ḥarakah on it, e.g.

عَنْ   مَنْ

At-tanwīn التَّنْوِيْن

A tanwīn is the extra nūn sākinah that comes at the end of a word, which is phonetically present and apparent in the state of waṣl, but is absent in written form and in the state of waqf.

A tanwīn is not written in the form of a ḥarf; its symbols are:

◌ٍ	◌ً	◌ٌ
كَسْرَتَيْن	فَتْحَتَيْن	ضَمَّتَيْن

To begin recitation with a tanwīn or repeat from it after a waqf is incorrect.

Nūn sākinah and tanwīn appear in 4 states:

1. Iẓhār
2. Idghām
3. Qalb
4. Ikhfāʾ

Al-iẓhār الإِظْهَار

Literal meaning: to make apparent.

Technical definition: to pronounce a letter clearly from its correct place (makhraj) with all its necessary qualities (ṣifāt lāzimah), and without any changes.

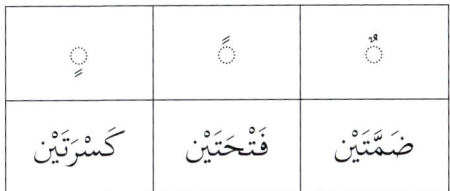

Rule: If any of the 6 ḥurūf ḥalqīyah appear after a nūn sākinah or tanwīn, the nūn sākinah or tanwīn will be pronounced with iẓhār (i.e. clearly, without ikhfā᾿ and ghunnah). This iẓhār is known as *iẓhār ḥalqī*.

Examples of iẓhār ḥalqī:

ء	مِنْ إِلٰهٍ	عَذَابٌ أَلِيْمٌ	هُوْدٍ أَوْ	مَرَّةً أُخْرٰى	
ه	يَنْهَوْنَ	فَرِيْقًا هَدٰى	إِنِ امْرُؤٌا هَلَكَ	بِخَيْرٍ هَلْ يَسْتَوِىْ	
ح	تَنْحِتُوْنَ	رِزْقًا حَسَنًا	شَيْءٍ حَفِيْظٍ	مَنْ حَادَّ	
خ	إِنْ خِفْتُمْ	نَارًا خٰلِدًا	يَوْمَئِذٍ خَاشِعَةٌ		
ع	أَنْعَمْتَ	مِنْ عَلَقٍ	حَقِيْقٌ عَلٰى	جَبَّارٍ عَنِيْدٍ	
غ	مِنْ غَفُوْرٍ	عَطَاءً غَيْرَ	فَسَيُنْغِضُوْنَ	مَاءٍ غَيْرِ آسِنٍ	وَعْدٌ غَيْرُ

Al-idghām الإِدْغَام

Literal meaning: to insert, incorporate, assimilate.

Technical definition: to combine one letter with another and recite with tashdīd.

Rule: If one of the letters of يَرْمَلُوْنَ appear after a nūn sākinah or tanwīn, idghām will be carried out on the nūn sākinah or tanwīn.

1) In lām and rā᾿, the idghām will be performed without ghunnah (idghām tāmm), e.g.

ل	مِنْ لَّدُنْهُ	وَيْلٌ لِّكُلِّ	ر	مِنْ رَّبِّ	بَشَرًا رَّسُوْلًا

This is also known as *idghām bilā ghunnah*.

2) In the rest of the letters (which can be remembered as يُوْمِن), the idghām will be performed with ghunnah[44] (idghām nāqiṣ), e.g.

ي	وَإِنْ يَّرَوْا	فِئَةٌ يَّنْصُرُوْنَهُ	و	مِنْ وَّالٍ	إِيْمَانًا وَّهُمْ
م	مِنْ مَّآءٍ	صِرَاطًا مُّسْتَقِيْمًا	ن	أَنْ نَّمُنَّ	مَلِكًا نُّقَاتِلْ

This is also known as *idghām maʿa ghunnah*.

3) There are four words in which there will be no idghām; instead, they will be read with iẓhār[45]:

دُنْيَا قِنْوَانٌ بُنْيَانٌ صِنْوَانٌ

This iẓhār is known as *iẓhār muṭlaq*.

Note: In يٰسٓ وَالْقُرْآنِ and نٓ وَالْقَلَمِ there are two ways to pronounce the nūn sākinahs in the case of waṣl:

1. With iẓhār, i.e.

   يٰسِيْنْ وَالْقُرْآنِ نُوْنْ وَالْقَلَمِ

   There is pronunciation of the nūn, and ghunnah will not occur.

2. With idghām, i.e.

   يٰسِيْ(نْ) وَّالْقُرْآنِ نُوْ(نْ) وَّالْقَلَمِ

   There is no pronunciation of the nūn, and ghunnah will occur.

---

[44] When ghunnah is mentioned in the context of idghām or ikhfāʾ, its duration is one alif.

[45] There will be no idghām here because the letters of يُوْمِن are in the same word as the nūn sākin, whereas idghām only occurs when the letters of يُوْمِن are in the word after.

According to Imām Ḥafṣ ﷺ, from the way of Imām ash-Shāṭibī ﷺ, both will be read with iẓhār only; according to Imām Ibn al-Jazarī ﷺ, they can be recited with both iẓhār and idghām.

Al-qalb الْقَلْب

Literal meaning: to change, turn, transform.

Technical definition: to change one letter into another.

Rule: If a bā᾽ appears after a nūn sākinah or tanwīn, the nūn sākinah or tanwīn will be changed into a mīm sākinah; ikhfā᾽ will then be performed on the mīm sākinah, with ghunnah[46], e.g.

مِنْۢ بَعْدُ سَمِيْعٌۢ بَصِيْرٌ

Al-ikhfā᾽ الإِخْفَاء

Literal meaning: to conceal.

Technical definition: to pronounce a letter with a sound midway between idghām and iẓhār.

Rule: If any of the 15 letters apart from the ḥurūf ḥalqīyah, the letters of يَرْمَلُوْنَ and bā᾽ appear after a nūn sākinah or tanwīn, ikhfā᾽ will be performed on the nūn sākinah or tanwīn, with ghunnah.

The edges of the tongue will slightly and very lightly touch the gums, so that the sound of ghunnah may emerge finely from within the ikhfā᾽, e.g.

يُنْفِقُوْنَ قَاعًا صَفْصَفًا مُنْذُ صَبْرٌ جَمِيْلٌ

This ikhfā᾽ is known as ikhfā᾽ ḥaqīqī[47].

[46] Please refer to *Ikhfā᾽ al-mīm as-sākinah* and the associated footnote in *Chapter 14*.

[47] According to many Arab scholars (particularly the Miṣrī and Shāmī qurrā᾽), the ghunnah sound in the ihkfā᾽ will be pronounced with tafkhīm if the nūn sākinah or

Chapter 16: Madd and its types

Literal meaning of madd (plural – mudūd): to extend, expand, spread, lengthen.

Technical definition: to lengthen/stretch a ḥarf al-madd or ḥarf al-līn.

As mentioned in Chapter 7, there are 3 ḥurūf al-madd:

ـِيْ = اِيْ   ـُوْ = اُوْ   ـَا = آ

The ḥurūf al-madd will be stretched for different lengths of time according to the madd types described in this chapter. There are three types of stretching:

1. **Qaṣr**: short stretch; its duration is one alif.
2. **Tawassuṭ**: medium stretch; its duration is 2, 2 ½ or 4 alifs.
3. **Ṭūl**: long stretch; its duration is 3 or 5 alifs.

Reciters should take care in fulfilling the duration of every madd, especially if they come across many mudūd in their recitation.

Types of madd

There are 2 types of madd:

1. Madd aṣlī
2. Madd farʿī

Al-madd al-aṣlī المَدُّ الْأَصْلِي / المَدُّ الطَّبِيْعِي

The sound of a ḥarf al-madd is stretched for such a duration, that without it the essence of the ḥarf al-madd cannot remain, e.g.

نُوْحِيْهَا

---

tanwīn is followed by a ḥarf mustaʿlī. The scholars of the South-Asian Subcontinent do not recognise this distinction, and according to them, the ghunnah sound will be pronounced with tarqīq in all cases.

There will always be qaṣr in reciting a madd aṣlī.

Stretching a madd aṣlī for more than one alif or less than one alif (in waṣl) is ḥarām, because prolonging for more than one alif adds a letter to the Qurʾān, and reducing to less than one alif removes a letter from the Qurʾān.

Even if a ḥarf al-madd is mawqūf (waqf is made upon it), it must not be stretched for more than one alif, e.g.

وَضُحٰهَا   تَوَّابًا   تَلٰهَا   أَعْلٰى

Al-madd al-farʿī الْمَدُّ الْفَرْعِي

When a hamzah or sukūn appears after a ḥarf al-madd, the sound will be lengthened further.

There are 4 types of madd farʿī that will be explained in this chapter:

1. Madd muttaṣil
2. Madd munfaṣil
3. Madd lāzim
4. Madd ʿāriḍ waqfī

1. Al-madd al-muttaṣil الْمَدُّ الْمُتَّصِل

If a hamzah appears after a ḥarf al-madd, in the same word, e.g.

جَآءَ   سُوْٓءَ   جِيْٓءَ

There will be tawassuṭ in this madd.

Madd muttaṣil is also known as madd wājib.

2. Al-madd al-munfaṣil الْمَدُّ الْمُنْفَصِل

When a hamzah appears after a ḥarf al-madd, in the next word, e.g.

إِنَّآ أَعْطَيْنَا   قَالُوْٓا اٰمَنَّا   فِيْٓ أَنْفُسِكُمْ

There will be tawassuṭ in this madd. According to some scholars, qaṣr is also permitted.

Please note: when performing waqf on a ḥarf al-madd that has a hamzah after it (in the next word), the ḥarf al-madd will not be stretched over the duration of one alif, e.g.

عَبَسَ وَتَوَلَّىٰٓ ۝ أَنْ جَآءَهُ الأَعْمىٰ ۝

Madd munfaṣil is also known as madd jāʾiz.

3. Al-madd al-lāzim المَدُّ اللَّازِم

When a sukūn aṣlī[48] appears after a ḥarf al-madd. There are 4 types of madd lāzim:

1. Kalimī muthaqqal
2. Kalimī mukhaffaf
3. Ḥarfī muthaqqal
4. Ḥarfī mukhaffaf

There will be ṭūl in all types of madd lāzim.

3.1 Al-madd al-lāzim al-kalimī al-muthaqqal المَدُّ اللَّازِم الْكَلِمِي الْمُثَقَّل

When a sukūn aṣlī appears after a ḥarf al-madd, in the same word, and that sukūn is muthaqqal ('heavy', due to the letter becoming mushaddad), e.g.

ضَآ(لْ)لَا = ضَآلَّا　　دَآ(بْ)بَةٌ = دَآبَّةٌ　　أَتُحَآ(جْ)جُوْ(نْ)نِيْ = أَتُحَآجُّوْنِّيْ

48 A sukūn that remains in both waqf and waṣl.

3.2 Al-madd al-lāzim al-kalimī al-mukhaffaf المَدُّ اللَّازِمِ الْكَلِمِي الْمُخَفَّف

When a sukūn aṣlī appears after a ḥarf al-madd, in the same word, and that sukūn is mukhaffaf ('light', as the letter stays sākin), e.g.[49]

آٰلْـٰٔنَ

3.3 Al-madd al-lāzim al-ḥarfī al-muthaqqal المَدُّ اللَّازِمِ الحَرْفِي الْمُثَقَّل

When sukūn aṣlī appears after a ḥarf al-madd, in the ḥurūf muqaṭṭaʿāt[50], and that sukūn is muthaqqal, e.g.

أَلِفْ لَامْ مِّيْمْ = الٓمٓ   الٓمٓصٓ   الٓمٓرٰ   طَا سِيْنْ مِّيْمْ = طسٓمٓ

In the beginning of Sūrat Āl ʿImrān, ṭūl or qaṣr can be applied to the mīm of الٓمٓ ۝ اللّٰهُ when doing waṣl between the two words.

3.4 Al-madd al-lāzim al-ḥarfī al-mukhaffaf المَدُّ اللَّازِمِ الحَرْفِي الْمُخَفَّف

When a sukūn aṣlī appears after a ḥarf al-madd, in the ḥurūf muqaṭṭaʿāt, and that sukūn is a mukhaffaf, e.g.

نُوْنْ = نٓ   قَافْ = قٓ   صَادْ = صٓ

كَافْ هَا يَا عَيْنْ صَادْ = كٓهيٰعٓصٓ

3. Al-madd al-ʿāriḍ al-waqfī المَدُّ الْعَارِض الوَقْفِي / المَدُّ العَارِض لِلسُّكُوْن

When a sukūn ʿāriḍī waqfī[51] occurs after a ḥarf al-madd, e.g.

تُكَذِّبَانْ ۝   يَعْلَمُوْنْ ۝   نَسْتَعِيْنْ ۝

---

[49] This is the only example in the Qurʾān; it appears in Sūrat Yūnus, verses 51 and 91.

[50] These are separate letters that form a verse. They are found only in the Qurʾān, and only Allah ﷻ knows what they mean.

[51] A temporary sukūn due to stopping.

In this madd, ṭūl, tawassuṭ and qaṣr are permitted. However, ṭūl is best, then tawassuṭ, and then qaṣr.

Madd ʿāriḍ waqfī also applies when waqf is carried out in the middle of a verse, e.g.

يَسُوْمُوْنَكُمْ سُوْٓءَ العَذَابِ يُذَبِّحُوْنَ أَبْنَآءَكُمْ

See *Chapter 21* for further waqf rules.

Note of caution

Each type of madd should be pronounced identically wherever it appears, e.g. if the reciter decides to recite a madd ʿāriḍ waqfī with ṭūl, then within that recitation session, all such madds should be recited with ṭūl.

Exercise: Draw a summary diagram similar to the one on p.73, writing only examples of each madd (not the name). Thereafter, close your textbook and label each example with its correct name, using your memory.

Extension task: The three other types of al-madd al-aṣlī (madd al-badal, madd al-ʿiwaḍ and madd aṣ-ṣilat aṣ-ṣughrā) have not been explained in this book. Research them, and present your findings to your teacher.

Chapter 17: Madd al-līn

As mentioned in Chapter 8, there are 2 ḥurūf al-līn:

◌َوْ   ◌َيْ

Madd al-līn is when a sukūn comes after a ḥarf al-līn.

There are 2 types of madd al-līn:

1. Madd al-līn lāzim
2. Madd al-līn ʿāriḍ

Madd al-līn al-lāzim مَدُّ اللِّيْنِ اللَّازِم

If a sukūn aṣlī (permanent sukūn) appears after a ḥarf al-līn, e.g.

كَافْ هَا يَا عَيْنْ صَادْ = كٓهيٰعٓصٓ   عَيْنْ سِيْنْ قَافْ = عٓسٓقٓ[52]

In this madd, ṭūl or tawassuṭ are permitted, but ṭūl is better.

Madd al-līn al-ʿāriḍ مَدُّ اللِّيْنِ الْعَارِض

If a sukūn ʿāriḍī (temporary sukūn) appears after a ḥarf al-līn, e.g.

خَوْف   صَيْف

In this madd, ṭūl, tawassuṭ and qaṣr are permitted. However, qaṣr is best, then tawassuṭ, and then ṭūl.

> **Exercise:** Find 3 further examples of madd al-līn in the Qurʾān.

---

[52] The ʿayn in كٓهيٰعٓصٓ is known as ʿAyn Maryam, and the ʿayn in عٓسٓقٓ is known as ʿAyn Shūrā.

Madd Summary Diagram

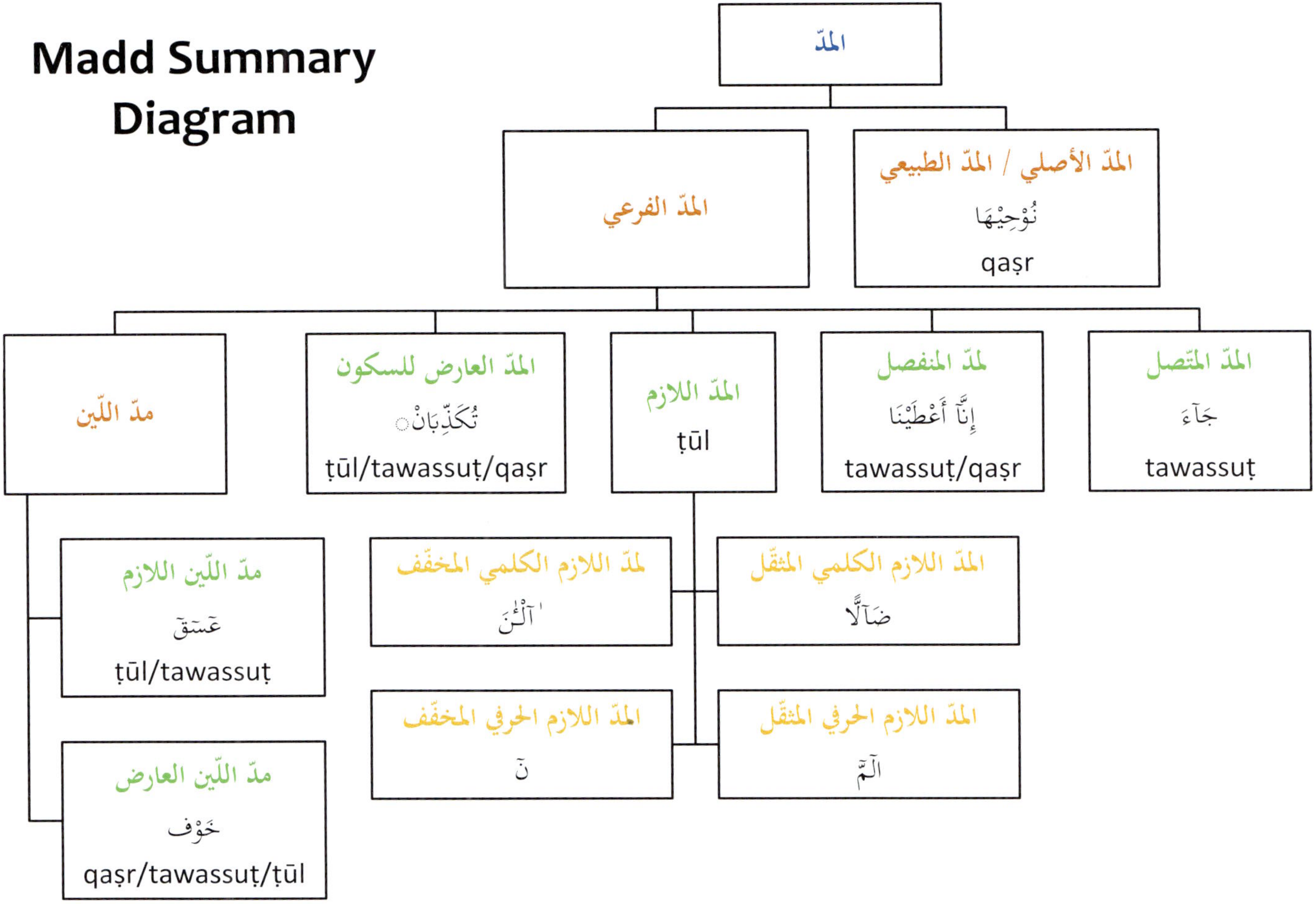

Chapter 18: The meeting of two sākins

Ijtimāʿ as-sākinayn اِجْتِمَاعُ السَّاكِنَيْن

When two sākins are next to each other, only the second one is pronounced with sukūn.

There are 2 types of ijtimāʿ as-sākinayn:

1. Ijtimāʿ as-sākinayn ʿalā ḥaddih
2. Ijtimāʿ as-sākinayn ʿalā ghayri ḥaddih

Ijtimāʿ as-sākinayn ʿalā ḥaddih اِجْتِمَاعُ السَّاكِنَيْن عَلىٰ حَدِّه

When the first sākin is a ḥarf al-madd, and both sākins are in the same word, e.g.

دَا(بْ)بَةٌ = دَآبَّةٌ　　　　(ءَا)لْٰئنَ = آلْٰئنَ

In آلْٰئنَ, the alif sākinah and lām sākinah are in the same word; in دَآبَّةٌ, the alif sākinah and bāʾ sākinah are both in one word.

This ijtimāʿ as-sākinayn occurs in waqf and waṣl, and a madd lāzim will be found in these places.

Ijtimāʿ as-sākinayn ʿalā ghayri ḥaddih اِجْتِمَاعُ السَّاكِنَيْن عَلىٰ غَيْرِ حَدِّه

When both sākins are not in the same word. There are 2 scenarios:

1) If the first sākin is a ḥarf al-madd and both sākins are in separate words, the first (ḥarf al-madd) sākin will not be pronounced, e.g.

فِيْ الكِتَابَة:	وَاسْتَبَقَا الْبَابَ	أَقِيْمُوْا الصَّلٰوةَ	فِيْ الْأَرْضِ
فِيْ القِرَاءَة:	وَاسْتَبَقَ الْبَابَ	أَقِيْمُ الصَّلٰوةَ	فِ الْأَرْضِ

The first line shows the examples in normal written form, and the second line depicts how they will be pronounced. So, in وَاسْتَبَقَ(ا) الْبَابَ the alif after the qāf will not be pronounced when doing waṣl.

2) If the first sākin is not a ḥarf al-madd and both sākins are in separate words, the first sākin will be given a kasrah[53], e.g.

قُلْ الْحَمْدُ ← قُلِ الْحَمْدُ   قُلْ الْحَقَّ ← قُلِ الْحَقَّ

Exceptions:

a) مِنْ (which is a ḥarf al-jarr) will be given a fatḥah, e.g.

مِنْ النَّاسِ ← مِنَ النَّاسِ   مِنْ اللهِ ← مِنَ اللهِ

b) When the first sākin is a mīm jam', it will be given a ḍammah, e.g.

عَلَيْهِمْ الْقِتَالُ ← عَلَيْهِمُ الْقِتَالُ   عَلَيْكُمْ الصِّيَامُ ← عَلَيْكُمُ الصِّيَامُ

c) The mīm of الٓمّٓ in the beginning of Sūrat Āl 'Imrān will be given a fatḥah in waṣl, e.g.

الٓمّٓ ۞ اللهُ ← الٓ(مِّيْم) اللهُ

If a hamzat al-waṣl[54] appears after a kalimah munawwanah (a word that has a tanwīn on it), the hamzat al-waṣl will not be pronounced and the tanwīn will be read as maksūr due to ijtimā' as-sākinayn 'alā ghayri ḥaddih, e.g.

فِيْ الْكِتَابَةِ:   خَيْرًا الْوَصِيَّةُ   خَبِيْئَةٍ اجْتُثَّتْ   بِزِيْنَةٍ الْكَوَاكِبِ

فِيْ الْقِرَاءَةِ:   خَيْرِنِ الْوَصِيَّةُ   خَبِيْئَتِنِ اجْتُثَّتْ   بِزِيْنَتِنِ الْكَوَاكِبِ

---

[53] السَّاكِن إذا حُرِّكَ حُرِّكَ بِالكَسْر – when a sākin is given a ḥarakah, it is (usually) given a kasrah.

[54] See *Chapter 20.*

Notice that in خَيْرًا الْوَصِيَّةُ, the alif written next to the fatḥatayn is not pronounced.

In the South African print of the Holy Qurʾān, which is widely used by non-Arabs, a small nūn is usually present to help the reader, i.e.

خَيْرَانِ الْوَصِيَّةُ   خَبِيْثَةِنِ اجْتُثَّتْ   بِزِيْنَةِنِ الْكَوَاكِبِ

This nūn is called the *nūn quṭnī*.

Exercise: Arabian muṣḥafs do not contain the nūn quṭnī. Look into one of these Qurʾāns and find 3 examples where you would normally use a nūn quṭnī to help you read correctly.

Extension task: Design a mini-poster displaying simplified rules and coloured examples of ijtimāʿ as-sākinayn. Stick this into your revision notes after it has been checked by your teacher.

Chapter 19: Imālah

Literal meaning of imālah: to incline, tilt, bend.

Technical definition: to incline (the sound of) a fatḥah towards a kasrah, or an alif towards a yā', thus reciting them in a majhūl manner[55].

There are 2 types of imālah:

1. Imālah mutawassiṭah
2. Imālah shadīdah

Al-imālat al-mutawassiṭah الإِمَالَةُ الْمُتَوَسِّطَة / الإِمَالَةُ الصُّغْرى

When the incline in the sound of a fatḥah towards a kasrah, or an alif towards a yā' is to a lesser extent. This is also known as imālah sughrā or at-taqlīl.

Imālah sughrā does not take place in the qirā'ah of Imām Ḥafṣ ﵀.

Al-imālat ash-shadīdah الإِمَالَةُ الشَّدِيْدَة / الإِمَالَةُ الْكُبْرى

When the incline in the sound of a fatḥah towards a kasrah, or an alif towards a yā' is to a greater extent. This is also known as imālah kubrā.

According to Imām Ḥafṣ ﵀, imālah kubrā will take place in Sūrat Hūd, verse 41:

بِسْمِ اللهِ مَجْرٖىهَا وَمُرْسٰىهَا

The original of مَجْرٖىهَا is مَجْرَاهَا.

---

[55]Imālah can best be understood when demonstrated verbally, especially the difference between as-sughrā and al-kubrā. Nevertheless, if imālah sughrā was carried out in the word شَاءَ, it would sound something like 'share' (in a northern English accent with no emphasis or pronunciation of the 'r'), and if imālah kubrā was carried out, it would sound like 'shay' (with a silent 'y'), rhyming with the last syllable of cafe.

It may be a good idea to look for authentic audio/video examples on YouTube if you do not have access to a tajwīd expert.

Chapter 20: The hamzah

There are 2 types of hamzah:

1. Hamzat al-qaṭʿ
2. Hamzat al-waṣl

Hamzat al-qaṭʿ هَمْزَةُ الْقَطْعِ / الهَمْزَةُ الْأَصْلِيَّةُ

This hamzah is an original part of the word and accepts all 3 ḥarakāt and sukūn. It must be pronounced clearly, and it remains as it is, even when the previous word is joined to it (in recitation), e.g.

إِنَّ أَكْرَمَكُمْ عِنْدَ اللهِ

Hamzat al-waṣl هَمْزَةُ الْوَصْلِ / الهَمْزَةُ الْعَارِضِيَّةُ

This hamzah is an extra part of the word, and occurs at its beginning.[56]

If recitation is commenced with a hamzat al-waṣl, it is pronounced clearly, but when the previous word is joined to it, the hamzah is not pronounced, e.g.

رَبِّ (ا)غْفِرْ لِيْ

1) If the hamzat al-waṣl is part of a noun, it will be read as a maksūr when it is pronounced, e.g.

اِنْتِقَامٍ　　اِبْنٌ　　اِمْرَأَةٌ

2) If the hamzat al-waṣl is part of an imperative verb, it will be read as a maḍmūm if the third letter of the word originallyhad a ḍammah on it[57], e.g.

---

[56] If you find it difficult to differentiate between a hamzat al-qaṭʿ and hamzat al-waṣl whilst reciting, look the word up in an Arabian muṣḥaf; if it is hamzat al-qaṭʿ, there will be a small hamzah above or below the alif (as is the convention in this textbook).

[57] In the muḍāriʿ original, because amr is made from the muḍāriʿ.

أُنْصُرُوْا أُعْبُدُوْا

3) If the hamzat al-waṣl is part of an imperative verb, it will be read as a maksūr if the third letter of the word originally had a fatḥah or kasrah on it, e.g.

اِعْدِلُوْا اِهْدِنَا اِعْلَمُوْا

This includes:

اِمْشُوْا اِرْمُوْا اِقْضُوْا

This is because the third letters were maksūr in the original form of these words:

اِمْشِيُوْا اِرْمِيُوْا اِقْضِيُوْا

4) If the hamzat al-waṣl is part of an alif lām at-taʿrīf, it will be read as a maftūḥ, e.g.

اَلْحَمْدُ اَلرَّحْمٰنُ

At-tashīl التَّسْهِيْل

When two hamzahs appear side by side, to pronounce the second hamzah from in between its own makhraj and that of the ḥarf al-madd that corresponds to its ḥarakah, e.g.

ءَأَنْذَرْتَهُمْ	the second hamzah is pronounced from between the makhraj of hamzah and alif maddīyah
ءَأُنْزِلَ عَلَيْهِ	the second hamzah is pronounced from between the makhraj of hamzah and wāw maddīyah
ءَإِذَا كُنَّا	the second hamzah is pronounced from between the makhraj of hamzah and yāʾ maddīyah

The hamzah upon which tashīl is carried out is known as a hamzah musahhalah.

According to the narration of Imām Ḥafṣ ﷺ, tashīl will only be carried out in verse 44 of Sūrat Ḥāmīm as-Sajdah (Sūrat Fuṣṣilat):

ءَاۨعْجَمِيٌّ وَّعَرَبِيٌّ

Note of caution

When pronouncing a hamzah sākinah, care must be taken that it does not change into an alif, wāw or yāʾ, e.g.

كَأْسًا ← كَاسًا　　مُؤْصَدَةٌ ← مُوْصَدَةٌ　　بِئْسَ ← بِيْسَ

Similarly, do not pronounce hamzah with tafkhīm, faintly, or with omission (i.e. missing the letter out completely).

Examples in which hamzah could be incorrectly pronounced with tafkhīm:

اَلطَّلَاقُ　　أَصْلَحَ　　أَصْطَفَىٰ

Examples in which hamzah could be incorrectly pronounced faintly:

اِهْدِنَا　　أَعْطَىٰ　　أَحَقُّ

Examples in which hamzah could be incorrectly pronounced with omission:

أَعُوْذُ　　اَلْحَمْدُ　　اَلسَّلَامُ

Exercise: Listen to a Qāriʾ who recites according to the narration of Imām Warsh ﷺ in order to understand how the three examples of tashīl are recited.
Hint: The qirāʾah of Warsh ﷺ is practised in Algeria, Morocco and Tunisia (amongst other countries).

Chapter 21: Waqf

Literal meaning of waqf: to stop.

Technical definition: to stop at a complete word (that which is separate from the word after it), for as long as one breath can be taken, with the intention to carry on reciting.

The word that is stopped on is called the *kalimah mawqūfah*.

There are 3 types of waqf:

1. Waqf bi ʿtibār al-maḥall
2. Waqf bi ʿtibār al-kayfīyah
3. Waqf bi ʿtibāri aḥwāl al-qāriʾ

Al-waqf bi ʿtibār al-maḥall الوَقْف بِاعْتِبَارِ الْمَحَلّ

The waqf in which the *place* of stopping is considered. There are 2 types of waqf bi ʿtibār al-maḥall:

1. Waqf jāʾiz – permissible stop
2. Waqf ghayr jāʾiz – impermissible stop

1. Al-waqf al-jāʾiz الوَقْفُ الْجَائِز

To stop at a place where the meaning is complete. There are 3 types of waqf jāʾiz:

1. Waqf tāmm – the complete stop
2. Waqf kāfī – the sufficient stop
3. Waqf ḥasan – the good stop

1.1 Al-waqf at-tāmm الوَقْفُ التَّامّ

To stop at a place where the meaning is complete, and the kalimah mawqūfah has no lafẓī[58] or maʿnawī[59] link with the word after it, e.g.

وَأُولَٰٓئِكَ هُمُ الْمُفْلِحُوْنَ۝ إِنَّ الَّذِيْنَ كَفَرُوْا

Translation: *'...and it is they who are the successful. Indeed, those who disbelieve...'* [2:5-6]

There is no need to repeat the kalimah mawqūfah when resuming recitation. Recitation will be started from the word after it.

When performing qaṭʿ[60], recitation should be completed at a waqf tāmm.

1.2 Al-waqf al-kāfī الوَقْفُ الْكَافِي

To stop at a place where the meaning is complete, and the kalimah mawqūfah has *only* a maʿnawī link with the word after it, e.g.

وَبِالْآخِرَةِ هُمْ يُوْقِنُوْنَ۝ أُولَٰٓئِكَ عَلَىٰ هُدًى

Translation: *'...and they believe in the Hereafter with certainty. They are upon (true) guidance...'* [2:4-5]

وَمَاهُمْ بِمُؤْمِنِيْنَ۝ يُخٰدِعُوْنَ اللّٰهَ

Translation: *'...and they are not (in fact) believers. They (seek to deceive Allah...'* [2:8-9]

There is no need to repeat the kalimah mawqūfah when resuming recitation.

---

[58] When the next words are part of the same sentence (grammatical link).

[59] When the next words are discussing the same topic (semantic link, i.e. link in meaning).

[60] To end a recitation, and then begin another activity. This can only be carried out at the end of a verse, and istiʿādhah must be recited before a new recitation session.

1.3 Al-waqf al-ḥasan الوَقْفُ الحَسَن

To stop at a place where the meaning is complete, and the kalimah mawqūfah has a maʿnawī *and* lafẓī link with the word after it.

If the waqf is at the end of a verse, recitation will resume from the next word, e.g.

فَمَنْ شَآءَ ذَكَرَهُۥ ۝ فِى صُحُفٍ مُّكَرَّمَةٍ ۝

Translation: *'So whoever wills may remember it, (it is recorded) in sheets held in honour.'* [80:12-13]

Otherwise, the kalimah mawqūfah will be repeated, e.g.

اَلْحَمْدُ لِلّٰهِ رَبِّ الْعٰلَمِيْنَ

Translation: *'(All) praise is (due) to Allah, Lord of the worlds.'* [1:1]

2. Al-waqf ghayr al-jāʾiz الوَقْفُ غَيْرُ الجَائِزِ

To stop at a place where the meaning is rendered incomplete, or against what Allah ﷻ actually said, e.g.

إِنَّ اللهَ لَا يَسْتَحْيِي أَنْ يَّضْرِبَ مَثَلًا

Translation: *'Indeed, Allah is not ashamed to present an example...'* [2:26][61]

يَٰٓأَيُّهَا الَّذِينَ اٰمَنُوا لَا تَقْرَبُوا الصَّلٰوةَ وَأَنْتُمْ سُكٰرٰى

Translation: *'O you who believe! Do not approach ṣalāh whilst you are intoxicated...'* [4:43][62]

---

[61] In this example, stopping at the word يَسْتَحْيِي would imply that Allah ﷻ is immodest, naʿūdhu bi 'llah.

[62] In this example, stopping at the word الصلوٰة would imply that Allah ﷻ is telling us not to pray ṣalāh, naʿūdhu bi 'llah.

وَتَرَكْنَا يُوسُفَ عِنْدَ مَتَٰعِنَا فَأَكَلَهُ الذِّئْبُ

Translation: *'...and we left Yūsuf with our possessions, and a wolf ate him...'* [12:17][63]

This waqf is not permissible in normal circumstances; if the reciter is forced to perform such a waqf (e.g. due to loss of breath), the kalimah mawqūfah *must* be repeated when resuming recitation.

This waqf is also known as waqf qabīḥ (repulsive stop).

Al-waqf bi ʿtibār al-kayfīyah الوَقْفُ بِاعْتِبَارِ الْكَيْفِيَّة

The waqf in which the condition of the last letter is considered. There are 3 types of waqf bi ʿtibār al-kayfīyah:

1. Waqf bi 'l-iskān
2. Waqf bi 'l-ishmām
3. Waqf bi 'r-rawm

Waqf may be performed on a word in any of these ways, as long as the rules pertaining to each type are followed.

1. Al-waqf bi 'l-iskān الوَقْف بِالْإِسْكَان

To simply make the last letter of a kalimah mawqūfah into a sākin.

This waqf occurs in the case of all 3 ḥarakāt, whether the ḥarakah is aṣlīyah (original) or ʿariḍīyah (temporary), single or tanwīn, e.g.

حَرَكَة أَصْلِيَّة: حَكِيْمٌ عَلِيْمٌ ۝ هُمُ الصّٰدِقُوْنَ ۝

حَرَكَة عَارِضِيَّة: عَلَيْكُمُ الصِّيَامُ مِنَ الثَّمَرَاتِ وَلَقَدِ اسْتُهْزِئَ

The tanwīn of the fatḥah will change to an alif, e.g.

---

[63] In this example, leaving out the word الذئب would totally change the sentence to mean: '...and we left Yūsuf near our possessions and he ate all of it (the food)'.

(نِسَآ) ← نِسَآءَا ← نِسَآءً عَلِيْمَا ← عَلِيْمًا

A tāʾ marbūṭah (ة), will change in to a hāʾ sākinah (hāʾ at-taʾnīth), e.g.

نِعْمَةٌ ← نِعْمَهْ

2. Al-waqf bi 'l-ishmām الوَقْف بِالْإِشْمَام[64]

To make the last letter of a kalimah mawqūfah into a sākin, in such a way that the lips indicate towards a ḍammah, i.e. they make the round shape that is seen when a ḍammah is pronounced[65].

This waqf only occurs on a ḍammah aṣlīyah and ḍammatayn, and does not occur on a ḍammah ʿariḍīyah, nor a tāʾ marbūṭah, e.g.

✓ ضَمَّة أَصْلِيَّة: وَهُوَ الْحَكِيْمُ الْخَبِيْرُ ۝ ضَمَّتَيْن: وَإِنَّمَآ أَنَا نَذِيْرٌ مُّبِيْنٌ ۝

✗ ضَمَّة عَارِضِيَّة: عَلَيْكُمُ الْقِتَالُ ة: إِذَا وَقَعَتِ الْوَاقِعَةُ ۝

3. Al-waqf bi 'r-rawm الوَقْف بِالرَّوْم

To pronounce the ḥarakah of the last letter of a kalimah mawqūfah in such a manner that people in close proximity can hear it[66]:

Rawm is the kind of light sound

That can be heard by the people around.

---

[64] حكمه حكم الوقف – the ruling of a word upon which waqf bi 'l-ishmām is carried out is that of waqf, i.e. its sound is pronounced in the same manner as it is pronounced in waqf bi 'l-iskān.

[65] Straight after pronouncing the maḍmūm letter as a sākin, the lips make the O-shape without making a sound; listeners who are unable to see the reciter's lips will not detect the ishmām.

[66] Only one third of the ḥarakah is pronounced; care must be taken not to add a hamzah after the ḥarakah. When waqf bi 'r-rawm is made on a tanwīn, one ḥarakah will be removed, and one third of the remaining ḥarakah will be pronounced.

This waqf occurs on a ḍammah aṣlīyah and kasrah aṣlīyah, and ḍammatayn and kasratayn, but does not occur on a ḍammah/kasrah ʿariḍīyah, nor a tāʾ marbūṭah, e.g.

✓ ضَمَّة/كَسْرَة أصْلِيَّة: اَلرَّحْمٰنِ۝ هٰذَا يَوْمُ الدِّيْنِ۝

✓ ضَمَّتَيْن/كَسْرَتَيْن: وَقَالُوْا مُعَلَّمٌ مَّجْنُوْنٌ۝ بِمَآءٍ مَّعِيْنٍ۝

✗ ضَمَّة/كَسْرَة عَارِضِيَّة: عَلَيْهِمُ الذِّلَّةُ قُلِ اللّٰهُمَّ حِيْنَئِذٍ

✗ ة: مَا الْحَآقَّةُ۝ فَأُهْلِكُوْا بِالطَّاغِيَةِ۝

When waqf bi ʻr-rawm is carried out, the kalimah mawqūfah is pronounced according to the same rulings as when it is recited in waṣl[67]:

1) The last letter will be recited with tafkhīm or tarqīq depending on how it is pronounced in waṣl:

	Waṣl	**Waqf bi ʻl-iskān**	**Waqf bi ʻr-rawm**
فَيَغْفِرُ	tafkhīm	tarqīq	tafkhīm
فِيْ لَيْلَةِ الْقَدْرِ	tarqīq	tafkhīm	tarqīq

2) Madd ʿāriḍ waqfī will not occur:

	Waṣl	**Waqf bi ʻl-iskān**	**Waqf bi ʻr-rawm**
إِيَّاكَ نَسْتَعِيْنُ	qaṣr only	ṭūl, tawassuṭ or qaṣr	qaṣr only

[67] حُكْمُهُ حُكْمُ الوَصْل – the ruling of a word upon which waqf bi ʻr-rawm is carried out is that of waṣl.

See *Appendix 3* for details about carrying out ishmām or rawm on a hā' aḍ-ḍamīr.

Al-waqf bi 'tibāri aḥwāl al-qāri' الوقف بِاعْتِبَارِ أَحْوَالِ الْقَارِئ

The waqf in which the condition of the reciter is considered. There are 4 types of waqf bi 'tibāri aḥwāl al-qāri':

1. Waqf ikhtiyārī – the voluntary stop
2. Waqf ikhtibārī – the test stop
3. Waqf iḍṭirārī – the forced stop
4. Waqf intiẓārī – the waiting stop

1. Al-waqf al-ikhtiyārī الوَقْفُ الاِخْتِيَارِي

This waqf is carried out in order to rest. In this case, the rules of al-waqf bi 'tibār al-maḥall will be considered.

2. Al-waqf al-ikhtibārī الوَقْفُ الاِخْتِبَارِي

This waqf is carried out by students when being tested by the teacher, in order for them to understand and learn the rules of waqf, and is carried out by the teacher so that they can teach and test their students about waqf.

3. Al-waqf al-iḍṭirārī الوَقْفُ الاِضْطِرَارِي

This waqf is carried out due to an excuse, such as running out of breath, coughing/sneezing, forgetting the next word, etc.

Sometimes, a waqf qabīḥ may occur. If this happens, the kalimah mawqūfah should be repeated when resuming tilawah, as long as an ibtidā' qabīḥ does not occur (see *Chapter 23*) – otherwise, it may be necessary to repeat a few words to make an ibtidā' jā'iz.

4. Al-waqf al-intiẓārī الوَقْفُ الاِنْتِظَارِي

This waqf is carried out repeatedly on one word, in order to demonstrate the different qirāʾāt (ways of reading).

See *Appendix 4* for details on waqf symbols.

Note of caution

If a ḥarf mawqūf is mushaddad, it must be pronounced properly in order not to resemble a sākin mukhaffaf, e.g.

عَدُوٌّ　　　　مِنْ نَبِيٍّ

The sound will linger on slightly, as can be differentiated in the examples below:

تَبَّتْ يَدَآ أَبِي لَهَبٍ وَتَبَّ ۝ مَآ أَغْنَىٰ عَنْهُ مَالُهُۥ وَمَا كَسَبَ ۝

إِنَّآ أَرْسَلْنَا عَلَيْهِمْ رِيحًا صَرْصَرًا فِي يَوْمِ نَحْسٍ مُّسْتَمِرٍّ ۝ تَنزِعُ النَّاسَ كَأَنَّهُمْ أَعْجَازُ نَخْلٍ مُّنْقَعِرٍ ۝

Exercise: Listen to a classmate reciting the Qurʾān; note down all the waqfs they make and identify the types.

Extension task: Summarise all the different forms of waqf, using a diagram form of your choice. Make sure to include explanations and examples in your chart.

Waqf Summary Diagram

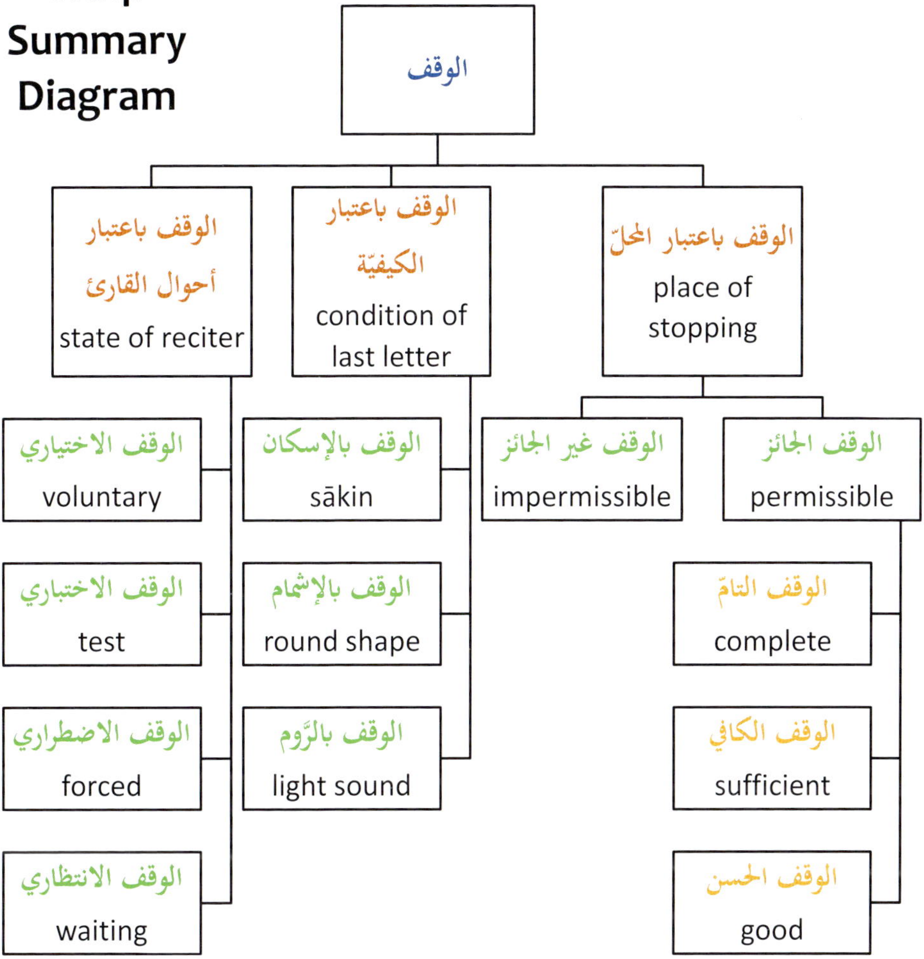
الوقف
الوقف باعتبار أحوال القارئ
state of reciter
الوقف باعتبار الكيفيّة
condition of last letter
الوقف باعتبار المحلّ
place of stopping
الوقف الاختياري
voluntary
الوقف الاختباري
test
الوقف الاضطراري
forced
الوقف الانتظاري
waiting
الوقف بالإسكان
sākin
الوقف بالإشمام
round shape
الوقف بالرَّوم
light sound
الوقف غير الجائز
impermissible
الوقف الجائز
permissible
الوقف التامّ
complete
الوقف الكافي
sufficient
الوقف الحسن
good

Chapter 22: Saktah

As-saktah السَّكْتَة

To stop a sound for a little while without breaking the breath. The rules that apply to waqf apply to saktah as well.

There are 2 types of saktah:

1. Saktah lafẓīyah
2. Saktah maʿnawīyah

As-saktat al-lafẓīyah السَّكْتَةُ اللَّفْظِيَّة

The saktah that is carried out on the sukūn of the letter before a hamzah, in order to pronounce the hamzah properly and clearly, e.g.

قَدْ أَفْلَحَ

(So that it is not pronounced as قَدَفْلَحَ)

As-saktat al-maʿnawīyah السَّكْتَةُ الْمَعْنَوِيَّة

The saktah that is carried out in between two words in order to separate the meaning, i.e. to ensure no confusion occurs in the understanding of the reader/listener.

According to Imām Ḥafṣ ﷀ, from the way of Imām ash-Shāṭibi ﷀ, saktah maʿnawīyah is wājib (necessary) in the state of waṣl in 4 places only:

1. Sūrat al-Kahf, verses 1-2: عِوَجًا **سكته** قَيِّمًا

   When saktah is carried out in عِوَجًا قَيِّمًا, the tanwīn of the fatḥatayn (ً) changes into an alif, i.e. it becomes عِوَجَا **سكته** قَيِّمًا.

2. Sūrat Yāsīn, verse 52: مَرْقَدِنَا **سكته** هَٰذَا

3. Sūrat al-Qiyāmah, verse 27: وَقِيْلَ مَنْ سكته رَاقٍ

4. Sūrat al-Muṭaffifīn, verse 14: كَلَّا بَلْ سكته رَانَ

When doing waqf on the words before the saktah symbol, the wujūb (necessity) of doing saktah is negated.

According to the way of Imām Ibn al-Jazarī رحمه الله, there is a choice whether to do saktah or not in the aforementioned 4 places.

Exercise: Learn the 4 wājib places of saktah by heart. There are other places where saktah may be indicated in some muṣḥafs, therefore it is important to know which ones are necessary.

Chapter 23: Ibtidāʾ

Literal meaning of ibtidāʾ: to initiate, to begin.

Technical definition: to start recitation after a qaṭʿ or a waqf.

There are 2 types of ibtidāʾ:

1. Ibtidāʾ jāʾiz
2. Ibtidāʾ qabīḥ

Al-ibtidāʾ al-jāʾiz الإِبْتِدَاءُ الْجَائِز

To start recitation from a place that conveys the correct meaning of a verse, in accordance with what Allah ﷻ intended. An ibtidāʾ after a waqf ḥasan is only permitted if the waqf was at the end of a verse.

Al-ibtidāʾ al-qabīḥ الإِبْتِدَاءُ الْقَبِيْح

To start recitation from a place that renders the meaning of a verse incomplete or incorrect, against what Allah ﷻ intended, e.g. to stop at وَقَالَتِ الْيَهُوْدُ and resume from يَدُ اللهِ مَغْلُوْلَةٌ in

وَقَالَتِ الْيَهُوْدُ يَدُ اللهِ مَغْلُوْلَةٌ

Translation: *'And the Jews say, "the hand of Allah is shackled"....'* [5:64]

An ibtidāʾ after a waqf ḥasan is not permitted if the waqf was in the middle of a verse, as this can ruin the intended meaning, e.g.

يُخْرِجُونَ الرَّسُولَ وَإِيَّاكُمْ أَنْ تُؤْمِنُوْا بِاللهِ رَبِّكُمْ

Translation: *'...having driven out the Messenger and yourselves because you believe in Allah, your Lord.'* [60:1]

Stopping at يُخْرِجُونَ الرَّسُولَ would be waqf ḥasan, but starting from وَإِيَّاكُمْ would be ibtidāʾ qabīḥ, as the words would then mean, 'be careful not to believe in Allah' (instead of '*...and yourselves because you believe in Allah*'), which is totally incorrect.

Chapter 24: Rasm al-khaṭṭ

Rasm al-khaṭṭ is the specific way in which the Qur'ānic text is written, according to the ḥadhf (omissions) and ziyādāt (additions) that conform to the consensus of the ṣaḥābah رضي الله عنهم.

For example, the words الرَّحْمٰنُ and الْعٰلَمِيْنَ (without an alif) are the spellings consistent with the 'Uthmānī script; if they were written as الرَّحْمَانُ and العَالَمِيْنَ in a Qur'ānic verse, it would be considered incorrect and contrary to rasm al-khaṭṭ.[68]

Silent letters

1) In some places in the Qur'ān, there are letters that are written but not pronounced, or only pronounced in certain situations:

Sūrah/verse	Word(s)	Ruling
Sūrat an-Naml, 27:36	فَمَا اٰتٰنِۦَ اللّٰهُ	The yā' in اٰتٰنِۦَ is pronounced in waṣl; in waqf, the reciter may pause on the nūn or the yā'.
Sūrat ar-Rūm, 30:10	أَسَآءُوا السُّوْٓاٰى/أَسَآءُوا السُّوْٓأَى	The yā' in السُّوْٓاٰى is silent.
Sūrat al-Ḥujurāt, 49:11	بِئْسَ الِاسْمُ	The alif of the word اسم is not pronounced; it will be pronounced as بِئْسَ لِسْمُ

[68] It is imperative to spell Qur'ānic verses according to the rules of rasm al-khaṭṭ. Such emphasis has been placed upon the preservation of the 'Uthmānī script, that it is impermissible to quote, write or print translations of Qur'ānic text without including the corresponding Arabic verses. See *Appendix 5*.

Sūrat ad-Dahr, 76:4	سَلَاسِلَا	The second alif of سَلَاسِلَا is not pronounced in waṣl; in waqf, the reader is permitted to recite it or omit it. The first alif will always be pronounced, in waṣl and waqf.
Sūrat ad-Dahr, 76:15-16	قَوَارِيْرَا۠ قَوَارِيْرَا	The second alif of the first قَوَارِيْرَا is not pronounced in waṣl; it is only pronounced in waqf. The second alif of the second قَوَارِيْرَا is not pronounced, neither in waṣl nor waqf.

2) In the following verses, there is a silent letter in the middle of a word:

Sūrah/verse	**Word(s)**	**Ruling**
Sūrat Āl ʿImrān, 3:144 & Sūrat al-Anbiyāʾ, 21:34	أَفَائِنْ/أَفَإِينْ	Pronounced as أَفَئِنْ
Sūrat al-Anʿām, 6:34	نَبَاى/نَبَإِى	Pronounced as نَبَإِ
Sūrat an-Naml, 27:21	لَأَاذْبَحَنَّهُ/لَأَاذْبَحَنَّهُ	Pronounced as لَأَذْبَحَنَّهُ
Sūrat al-Kahf, 18:23	لِشَاىْءٍ	Pronounced as لِشَيْءٍ

Sūrat al-Qaṣaṣ, 28:32 and a few other places Sūrat Yūnus, 10:83	مَلَائِهِ/مَلَإِيهِ	Pronounced as مَلَئِهِ The same rule will apply to مَلَائِهِمْ
Sūrat adh-Dhāriyāt, 51:47	بِأَيْيدٍ	Pronounced as بِأَيْدٍ
Sūrat aṭ-Ṭalaq, 65:4 & 65:6	أُولٰتِ	Pronounced as أُلَات
Sūrat al-Qalam, 68:6	بِأَيِيّكُمُ	Pronounced as بِأَيِّكُمُ

3) In the words below, the end alif is only pronounced in waqf, and not in waṣl:

Word	أنا (ضمير متكلّم)	ثَمُوْدَا	لِتَتْلُوَا	نَدْعُوَا	لٰكِنَّا	لِيَرْبُوَا
Verse	This pronoun is found in many verses of the Qurʾān	11:68, 25:38, 29:38, 53:51	13:30	18:14	18:38	30:39
Word		الظُّنُوْنَا	الرَّسُوْلَا	السَّبِيْلَا	لِيَبْلُوَا	نَبْلُوَا
Verse		33:10	33:66	33:67	47:4	47:31

4) In the South African print of the Qurʾān, there are a few places where لا is written, however the alif in the لا is not verbally pronounced[69]:

[69] In some later prints of the 13-line Qurʾān, the spelling has been standardised according to Arabian muṣḥafs, and this extra alif will not be found.

Sūrah/verse	Word(s)	Ruling
Sūrat Āl ʿImrān, 3:158	لَا إِلَى اللهِ تُحْشَرُوْنَ	Pronounced as لَإِلَى اللهِ تُحْشَرُوْنَ
Sūrat at-Tawbah, 9:47	وَلَا أَوْضَعُوْا	Pronounced as وَلَأَوْضَعُوْا
Sūrat aṣ-Ṣāffāt, 37:68	لَا إِلَى الْجَحِيْمِ	Pronounced as لَإِلَى الْجَحِيْمِ
Sūrat al-Ḥashr, 59:13	لَا أَنْتُمْ أَشَدُّ رَهْبَةً	Pronounced as لَأَنْتُمْ أَشَدُّ رَهْبَةً

In some muṣḥafs, a small circle (°) is placed on silent letters to show that they must not be pronounced during recital.

Added letters

There are some places where small letters are added, in order to help reciters pronounce certain words properly:

Sūrah/verse	Word(s)	Ruling
Sūrat al-Aʿrāf, 7:196	إِنَّ وَلِـيِّـىَ اللهُ	Pronounced as إِنَّ وَلِيِّيَ اللهُ
Sūrat al-Anbiyāʾ, 21:88	كَذٰلِكَ نُـۨجِى الْمُؤْمِنِيْنَ	Pronounced as كَذٰلِكَ نُنْجِي الْمُؤْمِنِيْنَ
Sūrat al-Furqān, 25:49	لِنُحْـِۧىَ بِهٖ	Pronounced as لِنُحْيِيَ بِهٖ
Sūrat al-Aḥqāf, 46:33 & Sūrat al-Qiyāmah, 75:40	أَنْ يُّحْـِۧىَ الْمَوْتٰى	Pronounced as أَنْ يُّحْيِيَ الْمَوْتٰى

Reading sīn in place of ṣad

There are 4 words in the Qurʾān that contain the letter ṣad with a small sīn above it:

Sūrah/verse	Word(s)	Ruling
Sūrat al-Baqarah, 2:245	يَقْبِضُ وَيَبْصُطُ	This will be pronounced as يَبْسُطُ
Sūrat at-Aʿrāf, 7:69	فِي الْخَلْقِ بَصْطَةً	This will be pronounced as بَسْطَةً
Sūrat aṭ-Ṭūr, 52:37	أَمْ هُمُ الْمُصَيْطِرُوْنَ	This may be pronounced as مُصَيْطِرُوْنَ or مُسَيْطِرُوْنَ
Sūrat al-Ghāshiyah, 88:22	بِمُصَيْطِرٍ	This will be pronounced as مُصَيْطِرٍ – thus in some Qurʾāns there will not be a sīn on top of the ṣad.

Exercise: Write down three verses of the Qurʾān from memory, then compare them to the actual text. How many errors did you make? Next time you recite the Qurʾān, look out for words that are written differently from their common (non-Qurʾānic) spellings.

Extension task: Rasm al-khaṭṭ is a crucial part of the preservation of the Holy Qurʾān.
Research the history of how the Qurʾān was compiled into written form, and make a timeline of the key events.

Chapter 25: Miscellaneous rules and guidelines

Sūrat Yūsuf لَا تَأْمَنَّا

In Sūrat Yūsuf [12:11], the word لَا تَأْمَنَّا was originally لَا تَأْمَنُنَا. Ishmām or rawm must be carried out on the nūn of this word to indicate towards its origins.

Method of ishmām: after pronouncing the first nūn (تَأْمَنْنَا) the lips will form a round shape, thus indicating towards the original ḍammah, then the second nūn (تَأْمَنْنَا) will be pronounced in the normal way. Idghām will occur.

Method of rawm: rawm will be carried out on the first nūn of لَا تَأْمَنُنَا, i.e. 1/3 of its ḥarakah will be pronounced. There will be no idghām[70].

Sūrat ar-Rūm ضَعْفٍ

In Sūrat ar-Rūm [30:54], the word ضَعْفٍ appears three times. It is best to recite this ḍād with a ḍammah, but fatḥah is also permitted.

Al-ḥurūf al-muqaṭṭaʿāt

When reciting the ḥurūf muqaṭṭaʿāt, the letters should be imagined as if they are spelt out, so that the various rules may be easily recognised, e.g.

طسٓمٓ = طَا سِيْنْ مِيْمْ ← طَاسِيّمِّيْمْ

Thus, idghām maʿa ghunnah will occur between the sīn and mīm, and a madd lāzim ḥarfī muthaqqal will also occur.

---

[70] When pronouncing with rawm, even though there is a nūn mushaddad in written form, the two nūns will not be combined verbally to form a nūn mushaddad; the word will be read as لَا تَأْمَنُنَا with rawm carried out on the first nūn.

The following tables shows the rules of عٓسٓقٓ and كٓهيعٓصٓ:

قَاف	سِيْن	عَيْن
المد اللازم	المد اللازم، الإخفاء	مد اللين اللازم، الإخفاء

صَادْ	عَيْن	يَا	هَا	كَاف
المد اللازم، القلقلة	مد اللين اللازم، الإخفاء	المد الأصلي	المد الأصلي	المد اللازم

Sajdat at-tilāwah

There are certain verses that require the reciter and listener(s) to prostrate after they are recited; such a prostration is known as sajdat at-tilāwah.

1) The words that make a sajdah wājib upon the reciter/listener are usually overscored, and the place where sajdah should be made are usually indicated via the اَلسَّجْدَة symbol[71], which can be found between lines or in the margins.
2) Within ṣalāh, the prostration must be carried out immediately; out of ṣalāh, it may be delayed, although it is preferable to perform it as soon as possible.
3) The sajdat at-tilāwah must be carried out in the state of wuḍū'; the same rules for purity of clothing and place, covering ʿawrah, etc. that apply in ṣalāh will apply to sajdat at-tilāwah.

[71] Sometimes the sajdah will be carried out one or two āyahs after the overscored text, i.e. in Sūrat an-Naḥl, 16:49-50; Sūrat al-Isrā', 17:107-109; Sūrat an-Naml, 27:25-26; and Sūrat Fuṣṣilat, 41:37-38.

4) The method of the sajdah is to stand facing the qiblah with the intention of performing sajdat at-tilāwah, and then go into sajdah reciting 'Allāhu Akbar' (without raising hands), and then rise from sajdah saying 'Allāhu Akbar' (with no salām thereafter).

5) A woman who was menstruating at the time of hearing a verse of prostration does not need to make a sajdah for it. Likewise, sajdat at-tilāwah only becomes wājib upon a listener if the verse is heard live, not from recordings.

There are many more rulings regarding the sajdat at-tilāwah that are more comprehensively covered in the books of fiqh.

Reciting in a pleasant tune

When reading the Qur'ān, as well as the rules of tajwīd, reciting in a pleasant tune is also commendable, as the Prophet ﷺ said:

إِقْرَءُوا الْقُرْآنَ بِلُحُوْنِ الْعَرَبِ وَأَصْوَاتِهَا

'Read the Qur'ān with the tunes and sounds of the Arabs.'

[Narrated by Ḥudhayfah ibn al-Yamān ﷺ, in al-Muʿjam al-Awsaṭ]

زَيِّنُوا الْقُرْآنَ بِأَصوَاتِكُمْ

'Beautify the Qur'ān with your voices.'

[Narrated by Ibn ʿAbbās ﷺ, in Musnad Aḥmad]

لِكُلِّ شَيْءٍ حِلْيَةٌ، وَحِلْيَةُ الْقُرْآنِ الصَّوْتُ الْحَسَنُ

Translation: *'Everything has an adornment, and the adornment of the Qur'ān is a good tune.'*

[Narrated by Ibn ʿAbbās ﷺ, in al-Muʿjam al-Awsaṭ]

وَآخِرُ دَعْوٰنَا أَنِ الْحَمْدُ لِلّٰهِ رَبِّ الْعٰلَمِيْنَ

Appendix 1: Importance of pronouncing letters correctly

All letters must be pronounced correctly whilst reciting the Qurʾān.

Mispronouncing letters can vastly change the meaning of verses and make the reciter sinful; it can also lead to the reciter's ṣalāh becoming invalid.

Care must be taken not to read one letter in place of another, especially in the following groups of letters:

ت ط	ث س ص	ح ه	خ غ	د ض	ذ ز ظ	ء ع	ق ك

Observe how the meaning changes in the following examples:

دَلَّ	he guided	ضَلَّ	he went astray
سَيْفٌ	sword	صَيْفٌ	summer
عَلِيْمٌ	All Knowing	أَلِيْمٌ	grievous, painful, excruciating
قَلْبٌ	heart	كَلْبٌ	dog
عَظِيْمٌ	great, magnificent	أَزِيْمٌ	root word means 'crisis, attack'
قُلْ	say	كُلْ	eat
اَلحَمْدُ لِلّٰهِ	All praise is for Allah	اَلْهَمْدُ لِلّٰهِ	death/fatigue/exhaustion is for Allah (naʿūdhu bi 'llah)
أَنْعَمْتَ عَلَيْهِمْ	(on whom) You have bestowed Your favour	أَنَمْتَ عَلَيْهِمْ	Sounds similar to: 'have you slept on them?'

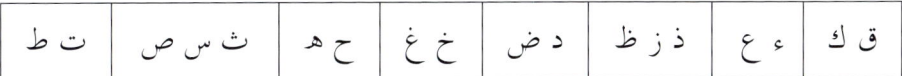

In the same way, substituting one ḥarakah for another can also change the meaning of word:

حُرٌّ	free, freeman	حَرٌّ	heat
ثُمَّ	then	ثَمَّ	there
جَمَالٌ	beauty	جِمَالٌ	camels
رَجُلٌ	man	رِجْلٌ	foot, leg

Appendix 2: Matan al-Jazarīyah[72]

مَنْظُومَةُ الْمُقَدِّمَهْ

فِيمَا يَجِبُ عَلَىٰ قَارِئِ الْقُرْآنِ أَنْ يَعْلَمَهْ

من نظم إمام الحفّاظ وحجّة القرّاء محمد بن محمد بن محمد بن علي بن يوسف **المعروف بابن الجزري** رحمه الله تعالى

The Poem of Introduction in what is Compulsory upon the Reciter of the Qurʾān to Know

Composed by Imām Ibn al-Jazarī ﵀[73]

Introduction – الْمُقَدِّمَةُ

يَقُولُ رَاجِي عَفْوِ رَبٍّ سَامِعِ مُحَمَّدُ بْنُ الْجَزَرِيِّ الشَّافِعِي

In the hope of pardon and forgiveness from the All-Hearing Lord ﷻ, Muḥammad ibn al-Jazarī ash-Shāfiʿī[74] ﵀ says:

الْحَمْدُ لِلهِ وَصَلَّى اللهُ عَلَىٰ نَبِيِّهِ وَمُصْطَفَاهُ

All Praise is due to Allah ﷻ, and may Allah's blessings be upon His Prophet ﷺ and Chosen One

مُحَمَّدٍ وَآلِهِ وَصَحْبِهِ وَمُقْرِئِ الْقُرْآنِ مَعْ مُحِبِّهِ

Muḥammad, and his family and companions, and the reciter of Qurʾān, together with the one who is devoted to it.

وَبَعْدُ: إِنَّ هٰذِهِ مُقَدِّمَهْ فِيمَا عَلَىٰ قَارِئِهِ أَنْ يَعْلَمَهْ

And thereafter: this is an introduction concerning which the reciter (of the Qurʾān) is required to learn.

إِذْ وَاجِبٌ عَلَيْهِمُ مُحَتَّمُ قَبْلَ الشُّرُوعِ أَوَّلًا أَنْ يَعْلَمُوا

[72] The Jazarīyah Poem – punctuation marks and word colouring are according to an old printed version of the poem; the translation follows the Arabic as closely as possible, but not word for word, as sometimes that does not make sense in English.

[73] Abu ʻl-Khayr Shams ad-Dīn Muḥammad ibn Muḥammad ibn Muḥammad ibn ʿAlī ibn Yūsuf al-Jazarī was an distinguished scholar of Kurdish origin whose works on tajwīd are considered classics. He was born in Damascus (Syria) in 751 AH (1350 CE); he grew up there and founded a madrasah called *Dār al-Qurʾān*. He travelled to Egypt a number of times, entered the lands of the Eastern Roman Empire, and travelled with Timur (Tamerlane) to Transoxiana. He then travelled to Shiraz (Iran), was made a judge, and passed away there in 833 AH (1429 CE).

[74] A follower of the Shāfiʿī school of thought in matters of fiqh.

It is obligatory, without any doubt, for them to know first before starting recitation:

مَخَارِجَ الْحُرُوفِ وَالصِّفَاتِ لِيَلْفِظُوا بِأَفْصَحِ اللُّغَاتِ

The articulation points and characteristics of letters, so that they can articulate in the most eloquent of languages,

مُحَرِّرِي التَّجْوِيدِ وَالْمَوَاقِفِ وَمَا الَّذِي رُسِمَ فِي الْمَصَاحِفِ

making clear the application of tajwīd and the stops, and that which is written in the (ʿUthmāni) copies of the Qurʾān,

مِنْ كُلِّ مَقْطُوعٍ وَمَوْصُولٍ بِهَا وَتَاءِ أُنْثَى لَمْ تَكُنْ تُكْتَبْ بِـ:هَا

with regards to all those words that are separated and joined in it (the written script of the Qurʾān), and the feminine tāʾ (ت) that is not written as a hāʾ (ة)

Articulation Points of the Letters – بَابُ مَخَارِجِ الْحُرُوفِ

مَخَارِجُ الْحُرُوفِ سَبْعَةَ عَشَرْ عَلَى الَّذِي يَخْتَارُهُ مَنِ اخْتَبَرْ

The articulation points of the letters are 17, according to (the opinion) chosen by the one who investigated[75].

لِلْجَوْفِ: أَلِفٌ وَأُخْتَاهَا، وَهِي حُرُوفُ مَدٍّ لِلْهَوَاءِ تَنْتَهِي

For the empty space of the throat and mouth are alif and its two sisters (wāw and yāʾ), and they are the madd letters that stop with the (stopping of) air.

ثُمَّ لِأَقْصَى الحَلْقِ: هَمْزٌ هَاءُ ومِنْ وَسَطِهِ: فَعَيْنٌ حَاءُ

Then from the furthest part of the throat are hamzah and hāʾ, from its middle ʿayn and ḥāʾ,

أَدْنَاهُ: غَيْنٌ خَاؤُهَا، والْقَافُ: أَقْصَى اللِّسَانِ فَوْقُ، ثُمَّ الْكَافُ

(From) its closest (to the mouth) are ghayn and khāʾ. The qāf (is from) the back of the tongue above (if the tongue is imagined vertically with the tip at the bottom), then the kāf

أَسْفَلُ، وَالْوَسْطُ: فَجِيمُ الشِّينُ يَا وَالضَّادُ: مِنْ حَافَتِهِ إِذْ وَلِيَا

[75] Imām Ibn al-Jazarī ﷺ is referring to Imām al-Khalīl ibn Aḥmad al-Farāhīdī ﷺ (718 – 786 CE), teacher of Imām Sībawayh ﷺ (c. 760 – 796 CE). However, research shows that the makhārij – although derived from Imām al-Khalīl an-Naḥwī and Sībawayh's works – were actually categorised into 17 types by a later scholar. Perhaps Imām Ibn al-Jazarī ﷺ is combining their collective research to make 17 categories.

is lower, and (from) the middle (of the tongue) is jīm, shin and yāʾ. The ḍād is from its (the tongue's) side when it is close

الَاضْرَاسَ مِنْ أَيْسَرَ أَوْ يُمْنَاهَا وَاللَّامُ: أَدْنَاهَا لِمُنْتَهَاهَا

to the molars, from its left or right. The lām (is from) its (the sides of the tongue's) closest part (to the mouth), until it ends (at the tip).

وَالنُّونُ: مِنْ طَرَفِهِ تَحْتُ اجْعَلُوا وَالرَّا: يُدَانِيهِ لِظَهْرٍ أَدْخَلُ

The nūn is from its (the tongue's) tip underneath (the lām - if the tongue is imagined vertically). The rāʾ is close to it (i.e. the nūn), but more towards the topside (i.e. the part of the tongue that connects with the upper palate).

وَالطَّاءُ وَالدَّالُ وَتَا: مِنْهُ وَمِنْ عُلْيَا الثَّنَايَا، وَالصَّفِيرُ: مُسْتَكِنّ

The ṭāʾ, dāl and tāʾ are from it (the tongue's tip) and the upper central incisors. The (letters of the) whistle (i.e. ṣād, zāy and sīn) emanate

مِنْهُ وَمِنْ فَوْقِ الثَّنَايَا السُّفْلَىٰ وَالظَّاءُ وَالذَّالُ وَثَا: لِلْعُلْيَا

from it (the tongue's tip) and from above the two lower central incisors. The ẓāʾ, dhāl and thāʾ are from the upper central incisors

مِنْ طَرَفَيْهِمَا، وَمِنْ بَطْنِ الشَّفَهْ: فَالْفَا مَعَ اطْرَافِ الثَّنَايَا الْمُشْرِفَهْ

from the edges of them both (i.e. the upper central incisors and the tongue). From the inner part of the (lower) lip is the fāʾ, along with the edges of the upper central incisors.

لِلشَّفَتَيْنِ: الْوَاوُ بَاءٌ مِيمُ وَغُنَّةٌ: مَخْرَجُهَا الْخَيْشُومُ

For the lips are wāw, mīm and bāʾ; and the articulation point of the ghunnah is the nasal cavity.

Characteristics of the Letters – بَابُ الصِّفَاتِ

صِفَاتُهَا: جَهْرٌ وَرِخْوٌ مُسْتَفِلْ مُنْفَتِحٌ مُصْمَتَةٌ، وَالضِّدَّ قُلْ

Their characteristics are *loud*, *soft*, *lowered* (empty mouth), *open* and *prevented*, and (for) the opposite (of them) say:

مَهْمُوسُهَا: فَحَثَّهُ شَخْصٌ سَكَتْ شَدِيْدُهَا لَفْظُ: أَجِدْ قَطٍ بَكَتْ

Their *quiet* ones are: فَحَثَّهُ شَخْصٌ سَكَتْ; their *hard* ones are أَجِدْ قَطٍ بَكَتْ.

وَبَيْنَ رِخْوٍ وَالشَّدِيدِ: لِنْ عُمَرْ وَسَبْعُ عُلْوٍ: خُصَّ ضَغْطٍ قِظْ حَصَرْ

Between the soft and hard ones are: لِنْ عُمَرْ; the 7 *elevated* (full mouth) ones are: خُصَّ ضَغْطٍ قِظْ.

وَصَادُ ضَادٌ طَاءُ ظَاءٌ: مُطْبَقَهْ   وَفَرَّ مِنْ لُبِّ: الْحُرُوفُ الْمُذْلَقَهْ

Ṣād, ḍād, ṭā' and ẓā' are *closed*; and فَرَّ مِنْ لُبِّ are the letters of the *edge* (of the tongue/lips).

صَفِيرُهَا: صَادٌ وَزَايٌ سِينُ   قَلْقَلَةٌ: قُطْبُ جَدٍ، وَاللِّينُ

The (letters of the) *whistle* are ṣād, zāy and sīn; the (letters of the) *echo* are قُطْبُ جَدٍ; the (letters of) *ease* are

وَاوٌ وَيَاءٌ سُكِّنَا، وَانْفَتَحَا   قَبْلَهُمَا، وَالِانْحِرَافُ: صُحِّحَا

wāw and yā' sākinah that have a fatḥah before them; *deviation* (from the makhraj) is correct

فِي اللَّامِ وَالرَّا، وَبِتَكْرِيرٍ جُعِلْ   وَلِلتَّفَشِّي: الشِّيْنُ، ضَادًا: اسْتَطِلْ

in the lām and rā'; and it (the rā') is made with *vibration* (in the tongue); for (the characteristic of) *spreading* is the shin; (and the final characteristic:) *prolong* the ḍād.

Tajwīd – بَابُ التَّجْوِيدِ

وَالأَخْذُ بِالتَّجْوِيدِ حَتْمٌ لَازِمُ   مَنْ لَمْ يُصَحِّحِ الْقُرَانَ آثِمُ

The practical application of tajwīd is without doubt compulsory; he who does not read the Qur'ān correctly is a sinner,

لِأَنَّهُ بِهِ الإِلَهُ أَنْزَلَا   وَهٰكَذَا مِنْهُ إِلَيْنَا وَصَلَا

because with it (tajwīd) the Lord ﷻ revealed it (the Qur'ān), and like this it reached us from Him (via Jibrīl ﵇, our Prophet ﷺ, the ṣaḥābah ﵃, etc.)

وَهُوَ أَيْضًا حِلْيَةُ التِّلَاوَةِ   وَزِيْنَةُ الأَدَاءِ وَالْقِرَاءَةِ

It (tajwīd) is also the adornment of recitation, and beautification of transmission and reading.

وَهُوَ إِعْطَاءُ الْحُرُوفِ حَقَّهَا   مِنْ كُلِّ صِفَةٍ وَمُسْتَحَقَّهَا

It (tajwīd) is giving each letter its (original) rights of every (inherent) characteristic, and (what became) its dues (acquired because of another characteristic),

وَرَدُّ كُلِّ وَاحِدٍ لِأَصْلِهِ   وَاللَّفْظُ فِي نَظِيْرِهِ كَمِثْلِهِ

and to pronounce each one (of the letters) from its origin, and (to pronounce) each word and its counterpart in the same way (in all places),

مُكَمَّلًا مِنْ غَيْرِ مَا تَكَلُّفِ   بِاللُّطْفِ فِي النُّطْقِ بِلَا تَعَسُّفِ

complete (with all its characteristics) without any exaggeration, with gentleness in pronunciation, and without any deviation.

وَلَيْسَ بَيْنَهُ وَبَيْنَ تَرْكِهِ   إِلَّا رِيَاضَةُ امْرِئٍ بِفَكِّهِ

There is nothing (no barrier) between it (applying tajwīd) and leaving it, except for a person to (correctly) exercise with his jaws.

Some Warnings – بَابٌ فِي ذِكْرِ بَعْضِ التَّنْبِيهَاتِ

فَرَقِّقَنْ مُسْتَفِلًا مِنْ أَحْرُفِ   وَحَاذِرَنْ تَفْخِيمَ لَفْظِ الأَلِفِ

Make tarqīq in the letters of istifāl, and beware of making tafkhīm in the letter alif (when it occurs after a letter of istifāl),

وَهَمْزَ: اَلْحَمْدُ أَعُوذُ اِهْدِنَا   اَللهُ، ثُمَّ لَامَ: لِلهِ لَنَا

(beware of tafkhīm in) the hamzah of: اَلْحَمْدُ, أَعُوذُ, اِهْدِنَا, اَللهُ; likewise the lām of: لِلهِ, لَنَا,

وَلْيَتَلَطَّفْ وَعَلَى اللهِ وَلَا الضْ   وَالْمِيمَ مِنْ: مَخْمَصَةٍ وَمِنْ مَرَضْ

(also) وَلْيَتَلَطَّفْ, وَعَلَى اللهِ, وَلَا الضَّآلِّيْنَ; likewise the mīm of: مَخْمَصَةٍ and مَرَضْ;

وَبَاءَ: بَرْقٍ، بَاطِلٍ، بِهِمْ، بِذِي   وَاحْرِصْ عَلَى الشِّدَّةِ وَالْجَهْرِ الَّذِي

Likewise the bāʾ of: بَرْقٍ, بَاطِلٍ, بِهِمْ, بِذِي. Take care on (implementing) the shiddah and jahr that are

فِيهَا وَفِي الْجِيمِ كَ: حُبِّ، الصَّبْرِ   رَبْوَةٍ، اجْتُثَّتْ، وَحَجِّ، الْفَجْرِ

in it (i.e. the bāʾ) and in the jīm, as in: حُبِّ, الصَّبْرِ, رَبْوَةٍ, اجْتُثَّتْ, حَجِّ, الْفَجْرِ.

وَبَيِّنَنْ مُقَلْقَلًا إِنْ سَكَنَا   وَإِنْ يَكُنْ فِي الْوَقْفِ كَانَ أَبْيَنَا

Make clear the letter of qalqalah when it occurs with sukūn, and if it occurs in waqf, it (the qalqalah) will be even stronger.

وَحَاءَ: حَصْحَصَ، أَحَطتُ، الْحَقُّ   وَسِينَ: مُسْتَقِيمِ، يَسْطُو، يَسْقُو

(Take care to read with tafkhīm) the ḥāʾ of: حَصْحَصَ, أَحَطتُ, الْحَقُّ; likewise the sīn of: مُسْتَقِيمِ, يَسْطُو, يَسْقُو.

Rāʾ – بَابُ الرَّاءَاتِ

وَرَقِّقِ الرَّاءَ إِذَا مَا كُسِرَتْ   كَذَاكَ بَعْدَ الْكَسْرِ حَيْثُ سَكَنَتْ

Make tarqīq of the rāʾ when it has a kasrah; likewise, after a kasrah, when it (the rāʾ) is sākinah,

إِنْ لَمْ تَكُنْ مِنْ قَبْلِ حَرْفِ اسْتِعْلَا   أَوْ كَانَتِ الْكَسْرَةُ لَيْسَتْ أَصْلَا

as long as it (the rāʾ sākinah) is not before a letter of istiʿlāʾ, or the kasrah is not original.

وَالْخُلْفُ فِي: فِرْقٍ، لِكَسْرٍ يُوجَدُ   وَأَخْفِ تَكْرِيرًا إِذَا تُشَدَّدُ

There is a difference of opinion in: فِرْقٍ, due to the presences of kasrah (on the qāf). Suppress the (characteristic of) takrīr when it (the rāʾ) is mushaddadah.

Lām, and Other Miscellaneous Rules – بَابُ اللَّامَاتِ وَأَحْكَامٍ مُتَفَرِّقَةٍ

وَفَخِّمِ اللَّامَ مِنِ اسْمِ اللهِ   عَنْ فَتْحٍ اَوْ ضَمٍّ كَ:عَبْدُ اللهِ

Make tafkhīm of the lām in the name 'Allah', when (the lām) is preceded by a fatḥah or a ḍammah, as in عَبْدُ اللهِ.

وَحَرْفَ الِاسْتِعْلَاءِ فَخِّمْ، وَاخْصُصَا   الِاطْبَاقَ أَقْوَىٰ نَحْوُ: قَالَ وَالْعَصَا

Make tafkhīm in the letter of istiʿlāʾ, especially the (letters of) iṭbāq (which) are stronger, like (the difference between) قَالَ and الْعَصَا.

وَبَيِّنِ الإِطْبَاقَ مِنْ: أَحَطتُ، مَعْ   بَسَطتَ وَالْخُلْفُ بِ:نَخْلُقكُّمْ وَقَعْ

Make evident the (characteristic of) iṭbāq (in the ṭāʾ) of: أَحَطتُ and بَسَطتَ; and there is a difference of opinion in (the presence of iṭbāq in): نَخْلُقكُّمْ.

وَاحْرِصْ عَلَى السُّكُونِ فِي جَعَلْنَا   أَنْعَمْتَ وَالْمَغْضُوبِ مَعْ ضَلَلْنَا

Take extra caution (avoid ḥarakah/qalqalah) on the sukūn of: جَعَلْنَا, أَنْعَمْتَ, الْمَغْضُوبِ and ضَلَلْنَا.

وَخَلِّصِ انْفِتَاحَ: مَحْذُورًا، عَسَىٰ   خَوْفَ اشْتِبَاهِهِ بِ:مَحْظُورًا، عَصَىٰ

Make clear the (characteristic of) infitāḥ: (in the dhāl of) مَحْذُورًا and (in the sīn of) عَسَىٰ, for fear of confusing it with: (the ẓāʾ of) مَحْظُورًا and (the ṣād of) عَصَىٰ.

وَرَاعِ شِدَّةً بِكَافٍ وَبِتَا   كَ: شِرْكِكُمْ وَتَتَوَفَّى فِتْنَةَ

Take care (to pronounce the) shiddah in kāf and tāʾ, as in: شِرْكِكُمْ, تَتَوَفَّى and فِتْنَةً.

وَأَوَّلَيْ مِثْلٍ وَجِنْسٍ إِنْ سَكَنْ   أَدْغِمْ كَ: قُلْ رَّبِّ وَ: بَلْ لَّا، وَأَبِنْ

If the first (letter) of two like letters and two similar letters is sākin, then make idghām, as in: قُلْ رَّبِّ and بَلْ لَّا. Make clear (without any merging)

فِي يَوْمٍ، مَعْ: قَالُوا وَهُمْ، وَ: قُلْ نَعَمْ   سَبِّحْهُ، لَا تُزِغْ قُلُوبَ، فَالْتَقَمْ

(the yāʾ in) فِي يَوْمٍ, along with (the wāw in) قَالُوا وَهُمْ, and (the lām in) قُلْ نَعَمْ, (the ḥāʾ in) سَبِّحْهُ, (the ghayn in) لَا تُزِغْ قُلُوب, (the lām in) فَالْتَقَمْ.

Ḍād and Ẓāʾ – بَابُ الضَّادِ وَالظَّاءِ

وَالضَّادَ: بِاسْتِطَالَةٍ وَمَخْرَجِ   مَيِّزْ مِنَ الظَّاءِ، وَكُلُّهَا تَجِي

Distinguish the ḍād with (the characteristic of) istiṭālah and (its) articulation point from the ẓāʾ, and all of them (all the ẓāʾ in the Qurʾān) come

فِي: الظَّعْنِ ظِلِّ الظُّهْرِ عُظْمِ الْحِفْظِ   أَيْقِظْ وَأَنْظِرْ عَظْمَ ظَهْرِ اللَّفْظِ

in (words derived from): الظَّعْن, ظِلّ, الظُّهْر, عُظْم, الْحِفْظ, أَيْقِظْ, أَنْظِرْ, عَظْم, ظَهْر, اللَّفْظِ,

ظَاهِرْ لَظَىٰ شُوَاظُ كَظْمٍ ظَلَمَا   أُغْلُظْ ظَلَامَ ظُفُرٍ انْتَظِرْ ظَمَا

ظَاهِر, لَظَىٰ, شُوَاظ, كَظْم, ظَلَمَ, اغْلُظْ, ظَلَام, ظُفُر, انْتَظِرْ, ظَمَأ,

أَظْفَرَ، ظَنًّا كَيْفَ جَا، وَعِظْ سِوىٰ   عِضِينَ، ظَلَّ النَّحْلِ زُخْرُفٍ سَوَا

أَظْفَرَ; ظَنًّا however it occurs (wherever and in whatever form); عِظْ except (in the word) عِضِينَ; (the word) ظَلَّ of (Sūrat) an-Naḥl and (Sūrat) az-Zukhruf are the same (i.e. contain a ẓāʾ);

وَظَلْتَ، ظَلْتُمْ، وَبِرُومٍ ظَلُّوا   كَالْحِجْرِ، ظَلَّتْ شُعَرَا نَظَلُّ

ظَلْتَ, ظَلْتُمْ; in (Sūrat) ar-Rūm: ظَلُّوا, like (in Sūrat) al-Ḥijr; ظَلَّتْ in (Sūrat) as-Shuʿarāʾ and نَظَلُّ;

يَظْلَلْنَ، مَحْظُورًا مَعَ الْمُحْتَظِرِ   وَكُنْتَ فَظًّا، وَجَمِيعَ النَّظَرِ

يَظْلَلْنَ, مَحْظُورًا, الْمُحْتَظِرِ, كُنْتَ فَظًّا, and all (forms of the word) النَّظَر

إِلَّا بِ:وَيْلٌ، هَلْ، وَأُولَى نَاضِرَهْ وَالْغَيْظُ لَا الرَّعْدُ وَهُودٌ قَاصِرَهْ

except in Wayl (Sūrat al-Muṭaffifīn), Hal (Sūrat al-Insān), and the first نَاضِرَة (in Sūrat al-Qiyāmah); (continuing with ẓā' words) الْغَيْظ, (but) not the short (ḍād) in (Sūrat) ar-Ra'd and (Sūrat) Hūd;

وَالْحَظُّ لَا الْحَضُّ عَلَى الطَّعَامِ وَفِي ظَنِينٍ الْخِلَافُ سَامِي

الْحَظّ, not (the one in) الْحَضُّ عَلَى الطَّعَامِ; and in ظَنِينٍ (Sūrat at-Takwīr, 81:24) there is a difference of opinion.

وَإِنْ تَلَاقَيَا الْبَيَانُ لَازِمُ: أَنْقَضَ ظَهْرَكَ، يَعَضُّ الظَّالِمُ

When the two (letters) meet, it is necessary to make (them) distinct, (as in) أَنْقَضَ ظَهْرَكَ and يَعَضُّ الظَّالِمُ,

وَاضْطُرَّ مَعْ وَعَظْتَ مَعْ أَفَضْتُمُ، وَصَفِّ هَا: جِبَاهُهُمْ عَلَيْهِمُ

and (make the ḍād/ẓā' clear in): اضْطُرَّ, وَعَظْتَ and أَفَضْتُمْ. Distinguish the hā' in جِبَاهُهُمْ and عَلَيْهِمْ.

Nūn & Mīm Mushaddadah, and Mīm Sākinah – بَابُ النُّونِ وَالْمِيمِ الْمُشَدَّدَتَيْنِ وَالْمِيمِ السَّاكِنَةِ

وَأَظْهِرِ الْغُنَّةَ مِنْ نُونٍ وَمِنْ مِيمٍ إِذَا مَا شُدِّدَا، وَأَخْفِيَنْ

Make clear the ghunnah of the nūn and mīm mushaddadah. Read with ikhfā'

الْمِيمَ إِنْ تَسْكُنْ بِغُنَّةٍ لَدَى بَاءٍ عَلَى الْمُخْتَارِ مِنْ أَهْلِ الْأَدَا

and ghunnah the mīm sākinah when it meets the bā', according to the preferred view of the scholars.

وَأَظْهِرَنْهَا عِنْدَ بَاقِي الْأَحْرُفِ وَاحْذَرْ لَدَى وَاوٍ وَفَا أَنْ تَخْتَفِي

Make iẓhār of it (the mīm sākinah) near the remaining letters (i.e. all letters except mīm and bā'), and be careful not to make ikhfā' (of the mīm sākinah) when it meets the wāw or fā'.

Rules of Nūn Sākinah and Tanwīn – بَابُ أَحْكَامِ النُّونِ السَّاكِنَةِ وَالتَّنْوِينِ

وَحُكْمُ تَنْوِينٍ وَنُونٍ يُلْفَى: إِظْهَارٌ، ادْغَامٌ، وَقَلْبٌ، إِخْفَا

The rules for tanwīn and nūn sākinah consist of: iẓhār, idghām, qalb and ikhfā'.

فَعِنْدَ حَرْفِ الْحَلْقِ أَظْهِرْ، وَادَّغِمْ　　　فِي اللَّامِ وَالرَّا لَا بِغُنَّةٍ لَزِمْ

Upon meeting the letters of throat make them (the nūn sākinah and tanwīn) *clear* (iẓhār). It is necessary to *merge* them into the lām and rāʾ (idghām) without ghunnah.

وَأَدْغِمَنْ بِغُنَّةٍ فِي: يُومِنُ　　　إِلَّا بِكِلْمَةٍ كَ:دُنْيَا عَنْوَنُوا

Merge them with ghunnah into (the letters of): يُومِنُ, except when they are in one word, like: دُنْيَا and عَنْوَنُوا.

وَالْقَلْبُ عِنْدَ الْبَا بِغُنَّةٍ، كَذَا　　　لِاخْفَا لَدَىٰ بَاقِي الْحُرُوفِ أُخِذَا

Qalb (*transforming* the nūn sākinah and tanwīn into a mīm) occurs when they meet the bāʾ, with ghunnah. Likewise, ikhfāʾ (*concealing* the nūn sākinah and tanwīn) is applied when they meet the remaining letters (i.e. other than the ḥurūf ḥalqīyah, lām and rāʾ, letters of يُومِنُ, and bāʾ).

Lengthening – بَابُ الْمَدِّ

وَالْمَدُّ: لَازِمٌ، وَوَاجِبٌ أَتَىٰ　　　وَجَائِزٌ، وَهْوَ وَقَصْرٌ ثَبَتَا

The (types of) madd (lengthening) are: lāzim, wājib and jāʾiz; and both (madd) and qaṣr (shortening) have been established (in madd jāʾiz).

فَلَازِمٌ: إِنْ جَاءَ بَعْدَ حَرْفِ مَدّ　　　سَاكِنُ حَالَيْنِ، وَبِالطُّولِ يُمَدّ

(Madd) lāzim: If after a ḥarf al-madd, (such a letter) appears that is sākin in both states (waqf and waṣl), it will be lengthened with ṭūl.

وَوَاجِبٌ: إِنْ جَاءَ قَبْلَ هَمْزَةِ　　　مُتَّصِلًا إِنْ جُمِعَا بِكِلْمَةِ

(Madd) wājib: If it (a ḥarf al-madd) appears before a hamzah, right next to it, in one word.

وَجَائِزٌ: إِذَا أَتَىٰ مُنْفَصِلَا　　　أَوْ عَرَضَ السُّكُونُ وَقْفًا مُسْجَلَا

(Madd) jāʾiz: When it occurs (a ḥarf al-madd before a hamzah) separately (in two words), or when a sukūn occurs (after a ḥarf al-madd) due to stopping (making waqf).

Knowing the Stops and Starts – بَابُ مَعْرِفَةِ الْوُقُوفِ وَالِابْتِدَاءِ

وَبَعْدَ تَجْوِيدِكَ لِلْحُرُوفِ　　　لَا بُدَّ مِنْ مَعْرِفَةِ الْوُقُوفِ

After your (knowledge of) tajwīd of the letters, it is without doubt necessary to have knowledge of the stops

وَالِابْتِدَاءِ، وَهْيَ تُقْسَمُ إِذَنْ　　　ثَلَاثَةً: تَامٌ، وَكَافٍ، وَحَسَنْ

and the starts. They (i.e. the stops) are thus divided into three (categories): tāmm (complete), kāfī (sufficient) and ḥasan (good).

وَهْيَ لِمَا تَمَّ: فَإِنْ لَمْ يُوجَدِ تَعَلُّقٌ – أَوْ كَانَ مَعْنًى – فَابْتَدِي

They (all three) refer to what is complete (in meaning); so, if there is no attachment (to what comes after it in meaning or grammar, i.e. waqf tāmm) – or it (the attachment) is in meaning (i.e. waqf kāfī) – then start (with what follows).

فَالتَّامُ، فَالْكَافِي، وَلَفْظًا: فَامْنَعَنْ إِلَّا رُؤُوسَ الآيِ جَوِّزْ، فَالْحَسَنْ

So, (that is) tāmm and kāfī. (If there is an attachment in meaning) *and* grammar, then prevent (from starting with what follows), except (when stopping) at the end of a verse, permit (to start with the beginning of the next verse); so, (this is waqf) ḥasan.

وَغَيْرُ مَا تَمَّ: قَبِيحٌ، وَلَهُ اَلْوَقْفُ مُضْطَرًّا، وَيَبْدَا قَبْلَهُ

What is not complete (in meaning) is qabīḥ (repulsive); it is allowed in a forced stop, and (the reciter) must start with what preceded it (i.e. resume recitation by repeating the last word).

وَلَيْسَ فِي الْقُرْآنِ مِنْ وَقْفٍ يَجِبْ وَلَا حَرَامٌ غَيْرُ مَا لَهُ سَبَبْ

There does not exist in the Qur'ān a stop that is necessary, nor a stop that is prohibited, except that which has a reason (for its necessity or prohibition).

Separated and Joined Words – بَابُ الْمَقْطُوعِ وَالْمَوْصُولِ

وَاعْرِفْ لِمَقْطُوعٍ وَمَوْصُولٍ وَتَا فِي الْمُصْحَفِ الإِمَامِ فِيمَا قَدْ أَتَى

Know the maqṭū' (those words that are written separately) and the mawṣūl (those words that are written joined together) and the tā' (ة that is written as a ت), in the leading muṣḥaf (i.e. the 'Uthmāni manuscript), as follows:

فَاقْطَعْ بِعَشْرِ كَلِمَاتٍ: أَنْ لَّا مَعْ: مَلْجَأَ، وَلَا إِلَهَ إِلَّا

Separate in ten words أَنْ لَّا (these words are written separately in ten places), with: مَلْجَأَ (Sūrat at-Tawbah, 9: 118) and لَا إِلَهَ إِلَّا (Sūrat Hūd, 11:14),

وَتَعْبُدُوا يَاسِينَ، ثَانِي هُودَ، لَا يُشْرِكْنَ، تُشْرِكْ، يَدْخُلَنْ، تَعْلُوا عَلَى

تَعْبُدُوا of (Sūrat) Yāsīn (36:60) and the second of (Sūrat) Hūd (11:26), لَا يُشْرِكْنَ (Sūrat al-Mumtaḥinah, 60:12), تُشْرِكْ (Sūrat al-Ḥajj, 22:26), يَدْخُلَنَّ (Sūrat al-Qalam, 68:24), تَعْلُوا عَلَى (Sūrat ad-Dukhān, 44:19),

أَنْ لَّا يَقُولُوا، لَا أَقُولَ. إِنْ مَّا: بِالرَّعْدِ. وَالْمَفْتُوحَ صِلْ. وَعَنْ مَّا

أَنْ لَّا يَقُولُوا (Sūrat al-Aʿrāf, 7:169), لَا أَقُولَ (Sūrat al-Aʿrāf, 7:105)[76]. (Separate) إِنْ مَّا (with a kasrah on the hamzah) in (Sūrat) ar-Raʿd (13:40), and (always) join the maftūḥ (أَمَّا). As for عَنْ مَّا:

نُهُوا اقْطَعُوا. مِنْ مَّا بِرُومٍ وَالنِّسَا خُلْفُ الْمُنَافِقِينَ. أَمْ مَّنْ: أَسَّسَا

separate in نُهُوا (Sūrat al-Aʿrāf, 7:166). (Separate) مِنْ مَّا in (Sūrat) ar-Rūm (30:28) and (Sūrat) an-Nisāʾ (4:25), and there is a difference (of opinion) in (Sūrat) al-Munāfiqūn (63:10). (Separate) أَمْ مَّنْ in أَسَّسَ (Sūrat at-Tawbah, 9: 109),

فُصِّلَتِ، النِّسَا، وَذِبْحٍ. حَيْثُ مَا. وَأَنْ لَّمِ الْمَفْتُوحَ. كَسْرُ إِنَّ مَا:

(Sūrat) Fuṣṣilat (41:40), (Sūrat) an-Nisāʾ (4:109), and Dhibḥ (Sūrat aṣ-Ṣāffāt, 37:11); (separate) حَيْثُ مَا (in Sūrat al-Baqarah, 2:144 & 2:150). (Separate) أَنْ لَّمْ (when the hamzah is) maftūḥ (wherever it occurs in the Qurʾān). (Separate) إِنَّ مَا (with the) kasrah (on the hamzah),

الْأَنْعَامَ. وَالْمَفْتُوحَ: يَدْعُونَ مَعًا وَخُلْفُ الْأَنْفَالِ وَنَحْلٍ وَقَعَا

(in Sūrat) al-Anʿām (6:134), and (separate) the maftūḥ (أَنَّ مَا) in both (occurrences of) يَدْعُونَ (Sūrat al-Ḥajj, 22:62 and Sūrat Luqmān, 31:30), and there is a difference (of opinion regarding أَنَّ مَا when it occurs) in (Sūrat) al-Anfāl (8:41) and (Sūrat) an-Naḥl (16:95).

وَ: كُلِّ مَا سَأَلْتُمُوهُ، وَاخْتُلِفْ رُدُّوا. كَذَا قُلْ بِئْسَمَا، وَالْوَصْلَ صِفْ

(Separate the كُلِّ مَا in) كُلِّ مَا سَأَلْتُمُوهُ (Sūrat Ibrāhīm, 14:34), and there is a difference (of opinion in the كُلَّ مَا of) رُدُّوا (Sūrat an-Nisāʾ, 4:91)[77]. Likewise (there is a difference with regards to بِئْسَمَا in) قُلْ بِئْسَمَا (Sūrat al-Baqarah, 2:93), and (the places where it is written) joined are as follows:

---

[76] There is one place not mentioned in the poem, in which there is a difference in opinion as to whether the أَنْ لَّا is written separately or joined: Sūrat al-Anbiyāʾ, 21:87.

[77] There are three places not mentioned in this poem, in which there is a difference of opinion regarding كُلَّ مَا: Sūrat al-Aʿrāf (7:28), Sūrat al-Muʾminūn (23:44) and Sūrat al-Mulk (67:8).

خَلَفْتُمُونِي وَاشْتَرَوْا. فِي مَا اقْطَعَا: أُوحِي، أَفَضْتُمُ، اشْتَهَتْ، يَبْلُوا مَعَا

أُوحِي :in فِي مَا Separate .(Sūrat al-Baqarah, 2:90) اشْتَرَوْا and (Sūrat al-Aʿrāf, 7:150) خَلَفْتُمُونِي (Sūrat al-Anʿām, 6:145), أَفَضْتُمْ (Sūrat an-Nūr, 24:14), اشْتَهَتْ (Sūrat al-Anbiyā', 21:102), and (after) both لِيَبْلُوَكُمْ (Sūrat al-Mā'idah, 5:48 and Sūrat al-Anʿām, 6:165),

ثَانِي فَعَلْنَ، وَقَعَتْ، رُومٌ، كِلَا تَنْزِيلُ، شُعَرَا، وَغَيْرَ هَا صِلَا

the second فَعَلْنَ (Sūrat al-Baqarah, 2:240); Waqaʿat (i.e. Sūrat al-Wāqiʿah, 56:61), (Sūrat) ar-Rūm (30:28), both (places in) Tanzīl (i.e. Sūrat az-Zumar, 39:3 & 39:46), (Sūrat) ash-Shuʿarā' (26:146), and besides these (occurrences) join (the rest).

فَأَيْنَمَا كَالنَّحْلِ: صِلْ، وَمُخْتَلِفْ فِي الشُّعَرَا الْأَحْزَابِ وَالنِّسَا وُصِفْ

Join فَأَيْنَمَا (Sūrat al-Baqarah, 2:115) like (أَيْنَمَا of Sūrat) an-Naḥl (16:76), and there is a difference (of opinion) described in (أَيْنَمَا of): (Sūrat) ash-Shuʿarā' (26:92), (Sūrat) al-Aḥzāb (33:61), and (Sūrat) an-Nisā' (4:78).

وَصِلْ: فَإِلَّمْ هُودَ. أَلَّنْ نَّجْعَلَ نَجْمَعَ. كَيْلَا تَحْزَنُوا، تَأْسَوْا عَلَىٰ

Join فَإِلَّمْ in (Sūrat) Hūd (11:14). (Also join the) أَلَّنْ (of) نَّجْعَلَ (Sūrat al-Kahf, 18:48, and) نَجْمَعَ (Sūrat al-Qiyāmah, 75:3). (Also join the) كَيْلَا (of) تَحْزَنُوا (Sūrat Āl ʿImrān, 3:153, and) تَأْسَوْا عَلَىٰ (Sūrat al-Ḥadīd, 57:23),

حَجٌّ، عَلَيْكَ حَرَجٌ. وَقَطْعُهُمْ عَنْ مَّنْ يَشَاءُ، مَنْ تَوَلَّىٰ. يَوْمَ هُمْ

(as well as in Sūrat) al-Ḥajj (22:5), (and the one before) عَلَيْكَ حَرَجٌ (Sūrat al-Aḥzāb, 33:50). (Separate) عَنْ مَّنْ (of) يَشَاءُ (Sūrat an-Nūr, 24:43, and) تَوَلَّىٰ (Sūrat an-Najm, 53:29). (Separate) يَوْمَ هُمْ (Sūrat Ghāfir, 40:16 and Sūrat adh-Dhāriyāt, 51:13).

وَ: مَالِ هٰذَا، وَالَّذِينَ، هٰٓؤُلَآ تَحِينَ: فِي الْإِمَامِ صِلْ، وَوُهِّلَا

(Separate the) مَالِ (from) هٰذَا (Sūrat al-Kahf, 18:49 and Sūrat al-Furqān, 25:7), الَّذِينَ (Sūrat al-Maʿārij, 70:36), and هٰٓؤُلَآ (Sūrat an-Nisā', 4:78). وَلَاتَ حِيْنَ (Sūrat Ṣād, 38:3) in the leader (i.e. the ʿUthmāni manuscript) is joined, but that (opinion) is weak (therefore, separate it).

وَوَزَنُوهُمُ، وَكَالُوهُمْ صِلِ كَذَا مِنَ: الْ، وَيَا، وَهَا، لَا تَفْصِلِ

Join (the هُمْ of) وَزَنُوهُمْ and كَالُوهُمْ (in Sūrat al-Muṭaffifīn, 83:3). Likewise, (join the) الْ, يٰ,

and هٰ, (and) do not separate (from what comes after, e.g. in the word هٰذَا).

Tāʾ – بَابُ التَّاءَاتِ

وَرَحْمَتُ الزُّخْرُفِ بِالتَّا زَبَرَهْ   الَاعْرَافِ رُومٍ هُودَ كَافَ الْبَقَرَهْ

(The word) رَحْمَتَ in (Sūrat) az-Zukhruf (43:32) is written with a ت (not a ة); (likewise in Sūrat) al-Aʿrāf (7:56), (Sūrat) ar-Rūm (30:50), (Sūrat) Hūd (11:73), Kāf (Sūrat Maryam, 19:2), and (Sūrat) al-Baqarah (2:218).

نِعْمَتُهَا، ثَلَاثُ نَحْلٍ، إِبْرَهَمْ   مَعًا: أَخِيرَاتٌ، عُقُودُ الثَّانِ: هَمّْ

(Also written with a ت is) its last نِعْمَت (i.e. Sūrat al-Baqarah, 2:231), the last three (places) of (Sūrat) an-Naḥl (16:72, 16:83 & 16:114), the last two (places) of (Sūrat) Ibrāhīm (14:28 & 14:34), and the second (place in) ʿUqūd (Sūrat al-Māʾidah, 5:11, where it comes before the word) هَمّ.

لُقْمَانُ، ثُمَّ فَاطِرٌ، كَالطُّورِ   عِمْرَانَ. لَعْنَتَ: بِهَا، وَالنُّورِ

(Likewise the word نِعْمَت in Sūrat) Luqmān (31:31), then (Sūrat) Fāṭir (35:3), like (Sūrat) aṭ-Ṭūr (52:29), and (Sūrat Āl) ʿImrān (3:103). (Also written with a ت is) لَعْنَت in it (i.e. Sūrat Āl ʿImrān, 3:61) and (Sūrat) an-Nūr (24:7).

وَامْرَأَتٌ: يُوسُفَ، عِمْرَانَ، الْقَصَصْ   تَحْرِيمُ. مَعْصِيَتْ: بِقَدْ سَمِعْ يُخَصْ

(Also written with a ت is the word) امْرَأَت in: (Sūrat) Yūsuf (12:30 & 12:51), (Sūrat Āl) ʿImrān (3:35), (Sūrat) al-Qaṣaṣ (28:9), and (three places in Sūrat) at-Taḥrīm (66:10 & 66:11). (Also written with a ت is) مَعْصِيَت in Qad Samiʿ (i.e. Sūrat al-Mujādalah, 58:8 & 58:9).

شَجَرَتَ: الدُّخَانِ. سُنَّتْ: فَاطِرِ   كُلًّا، وَالَانْفَالِ، وَأُخْرىٰ غَافِرِ

(Also written with a ت is) شَجَرَت in (Sūrat) ad-Dukhān (44:43). (Likewise) سُنَّت in all (three places in Sūrat) Fāṭir (35:43), (Sūrat) al-Anfāl (8:38), and the last (occurrence) of (Sūrat) Ghāfir (40:85).

قُرَّتُ عَيْنٍ. جَنَّتٌ: فِي وَقَعَتْ   فِطْرَتْ. بَقِيَّتْ. وَابْنَتٌ. وَكَلِمَتْ

(Also written with a ت are the following words) قُرَّتُ عَيْنٍ (in Sūrat al-Qaṣaṣ, 28:9); جَنَّت in Waqaʿat (i.e. Sūrat al-Wāqiʿah, 56:89); فِطْرَت (in Sūrat ar-Rūm, 30:30); بَقِيَّت (in Sūrat Hūd, 11:86); ابْنَت (in Sūrat at-Taḥrīm, 66:12); and كَلِمَت

أَوْسَطَ الاَعْرَافِ. وَكُلُّ مَا اخْتُلِفْ   جَمْعًا وَفَرْدًا فِيهِ: بِالتَّاءِ عُرِفْ

in the middle of (Sūrat) al-Aʿrāf (7:137). And all (words) in which there is a difference (in opinion), in terms of being plural or singular, is known to be (written) with a ت.[78]

Hamzat al-Waṣl – بَابُ هَمْزِ الوَصْلِ

وَابْدَأْ بِهَمْزِ الْوَصْلِ مِنْ فِعْلٍ بِضَمّ   إِنْ كَانَ ثَالِثٌ مِنَ الْفِعْلِ يُضَمّ

Start on the hamzat al-waṣl (at the beginning) of a verb with a ḍammah, if the third letter of the verb has a ḍammah.

وَاكْسِرْهُ حَالَ الْكَسْرِ وَالْفَتْحِ، وَفِي   الاَسْمَاءِ غَيْرَ اللَّامِ كَسْرُهَا، وَفِي:

Give it (the hamzat al-waṣl) a kasrah (when the third letter of the verb is) in the state of kasrah or fatḥah. In nouns without the (alif) lām (at the beginning), it (the hamzat al-waṣl) will have a kasrah. And (the hamzat al-waṣl will also start with a kasrah) in (the following irregular nouns):

ابْنٍ، مَعَ ابْنَةٍ، امْرِئٍ، وَاثْنَيْنِ   وَامْرَأَةٍ، وَاسْمٍ، مَعَ اثْنَتَيْنِ

ابْن, ابْنَة, امْرِئ, اثْنَيْن, امْرَأَة, اسْم and اثْنَتَيْن.

Stopping on the Ends of Words – بَابُ الوَقْفِ عَلَىٰ أَوَاخِرِ الكَلِمِ

وَحَاذِرِ الْوَقْفَ بِكُلِّ الْحَرَكَهْ   إِلَّا إِذَا رُمْتَ فَبَعْضُ الْحَرَكَهْ

Beware of stopping with a full vowel sound; unless you are carrying out a waqf bi ʻr-rawm, then (pronounce) part of the ḥarakah,

إِلَّا بِفَتْحٍ أَوْ بِنَصْبٍ، وَأَشِمّ   إِشَارَةً بِالضَّمِّ: فِي رَفْعٍ وَضَمّ

[78] This occurs in 12 places, as compiled in the following poem:

وكل ما فيه الخلاف يجري...جمعا وفردا فبتاء فادر   وذا: جملت، وآيت، أتى...في يوسف والعنكبوت يا فتى

وكلمت: وهو في الطول مع...أنعامه ثم بيونس معا   والغرفت: في سبأ، وبينت:...في فاطر، وثمرت فصلت

(The āyah references are as follows: 7:33, 12:7, 29:50, 6:115, 10:33, 10:96, 40:6, 34:37, 35:40, 41:47, 12:10 and 12:15.)

except (there will be no waqf bi ʻr-rawm) on a fatḥah or a naṣb. Implement ishmām by indicating towards a ḍammah (using the lips), in the (last letter being in the) state of rafʿ or ḍammah.

The End – الخَاتِمَةُ

وَقَدْ تَقَضّٰى نَظْمِيَ: الْمُقَدِّمَهْ   مِنِّي لِقَارِئِ الْقُرَانِ تَقْدِمَهْ

My poem of introduction has come to an end, a present from me to the reciter of the Qurʾān.

[أَبْيَاتُهَا قَافٌ وَزَايٌ فِي الْعَدَدْ   مَنْ يُحْسِنِ التَّجْوِيدَ يَظْفَرْ بِالرَّشَدْ][79]

Its couplets are qāf and zāy in number[80]. Whosoever beautifully implements tajwīd will achieve true guidance.

وَالْحَمْدُ لِلّٰهِ لَهَا خِتَامُ   ثُمَّ الصَّلَاةُ بَعْدُ وَالسَّلَامُ

All Praise is due to Allah for the conclusion (of this poem), thereafter Blessings and Peace

[عَلَى النَّبِيِّ الْمُصْطَفَى وَآلِهِ   وَصَحْبِهِ وتَابِعِي مِنْوَالِهِ]

upon the Chosen Prophet ﷺ, his family and companions, and those who follow his example.

تَمَّتِ الْمَنْظُومَةُ وَالْحَمْدُ لِلّٰهِ رَبِّ الْعٰلَمِينَ

---

[79] The bracketed couplets were added by later scholars and are not part of the original poem.

[80] The Arabs used letters to represent numbers before the Hindu-Arabic numerals were adopted in Arabia. This is known as the ʻAbjadʼ system, after the order of letters represented by the following sentence:

اَبْجَدْ هَوَّزْ حُطِّيْ كَلَمَنْ سَعْفَصْ قَرَشَتْ ثَخَذْ ضَظَغْ

The value of each letter is shown below:

ن	م	ل	ك	ي	ط	ح	ز	و	ه	د	ج	ب	ا
50	40	30	20	10	9	8	7	6	5	4	3	2	1
غ	ظ	ض	ذ	خ	ث	ت	ش	ر	ق	ص	ف	ع	س
1000	900	800	700	600	500	400	300	200	100	90	80	70	60

Fun fact: if you add up the value of all the letters in the basmalah, you will get a total of 786.

Appendix 3: Madhhab at-tafṣīl

There are 3 schools of thought with regards to carrying out ishmām or rawm on hāʾ aḍ-ḍamīr (wāḥid mudhakkar ghāʾib).

1. **Madhhab al-manʿ** مَذْهَبُ الْمَنْع

General prohibition of ishmām or rawm, based on the similarity of a hāʾ aḍ-ḍamīr to a hāʾ at-taʾnīth in the state of waqf.

2. **Madhhab al-jawāz** مَذْهَبُ الْجَوَاز

General permission, when the rules of ishmām or rawm (mentioned in *Chapter 21*) are adhered to.

3. **Madhhab at-tafṣīl** مَذْهَبُ التَّفْصِيْل

The majority opinion (also the one preferred by Imām Ibn al-Jazarī رحمه الله) is that ishmām or rawm on a hāʾ aḍ-ḍamīr is prohibited in 4 states:

1) When a hāʾ aḍ-ḍamīr has a yāʾ sākinah before it, e.g. فِيْهِ
2) When a hāʾ aḍ-ḍamīr has a wāw sākinah before it, e.g. فَعَلُوْهُ
3) When a hāʾ aḍ-ḍamīr has a kasrah before it, e.g. وَكُتُبِهِ
4) When a hāʾ aḍ-ḍamīr has a ḍammah before it, e.g. يُخْلِفُهُ

Ishmām or rawm on a hāʾ aḍ-ḍamīr is permitted in 3 cases:

1) When a hāʾ aḍ-ḍamīr has a fatḥah before it, e.g. لَنْ تُخْلَفَهُ
2) When a hāʾ aḍ-ḍamīr has a sukūn aṣlī before it, e.g. مِنْهُ
3) When a hāʾ aḍ-ḍamīr has an alif before it, e.g. فَاجْتَبٰهُ

Appendix 4: Symbols of waqf and waṣl

The following symbols are found in the South African Qur'ān (the shaded ones are also found in the Arabian muṣḥafs):

Symbol	Meaning	Rule
○	وَقْف تَامّ Perfect stop	This symbol indicates the end of a verse. At this point, the meaning is complete and reciter should stop and take a breath before continuing. It is **preferable to stop**, not compulsory, because sometimes there is still a grammatical link with the following verse. Originally, this symbol was denoted by a ة but is now simply indicated by a circle.
م	وَقْف لَازِم Compulsory stop	It is **compulsory to stop** here; doing waṣl will drastically change the meaning of the verse.
ج	وَقْف جَائِز Permissible stop	This symbol indicates towards the completion of a matter discussed in that fragment of the verse. It is **better to stop** to create a good effect, however it is **also fine to continue**.
لا	لَا وَقْف عَلَيْه Impermissible stop	It is **not permissible to stop** here, as stopping can change the meaning or context of the verse.

◌ۛ	وَقْف مُعَانَقَه Embracing stop	This triple dot symbol will occur in pairs close to each other. There may also be a مع written in the margins of the script. The reciter **must do waqf at one symbol and do waṣl at the other**. Stopping at both symbols will isolate the middle sentence from both the sentences on either side, causing a nonsensical meaning. Continuing at both symbols will cause a confusion in the meaning. Thus, one can stop at either one of the two symbols, but not both.
۵	آيَة مُخْتَلَف فِيْهَا Non-Kūfī āyah	This symbol indicates a point where there are differing opinions as to whether it is the end of a verse or not. It carries the same rule as the 'perfect stop' denoted by a circle.
ط	وَقْف مُطْلَق Absolute stop	It is **best to stop** here, as continuing could cause a weakness in the meaning. This stop differs from the 'perfect stop' in that the full sentence has not yet been completed, and there is still something to follow before the matter is completely discussed.
قلے ◌	الوَقْف أَوْلىٰ Waqf is better	It is **best to stop,** but also permissible to continue.

صلے	الوَصْل أَوْلیٰ Waṣl is better	It is **best to do waṣl**, but also permissible to stop. If the reciter stops here, then they should repeat the kalimah mawqūfah when resuming recitation.
ز	وَقْف مُجَوَّز Accepted pause	It is **better to do waṣl**, although it is permissible to stop if the reciter needs to take a breath.
ص	وَقْف مُرَخَّص Licensed pause	It is **better to do waṣl**, although it is permissible to stop if the reciter needs to take a breath. It is more desirable to continue at this symbol than at ز .
قَف	قَدْ يُوْقَف Waqf has been done upon it	It is **better to do waṣl**, but permissible to stop for a valid reason.
صَل	قَدْ يُوْصَل Waṣl has been done upon it	It is **better to do waṣl**, but permissible to stop.
ق	قِيْلَ عَلَيْهِ الْوَقْف It is said there is waqf here	This symbol indicates differing opinions on whether to stop or not. It is **permissible to stop** but **better to continue**.

قِلا	قِيْلَ لا وَقْف عَلَيْهِ It is said there is no waqf here	This symbol indicates differing opinions on whether to stop or not. It is **better to continue** according to the majority of scholars.
ك	كَذٰلِك The same as before	The rule here is same as the waqf symbol that came before it.
لا ۝	آية لَا وَقْف عَلَيْه Verse with no waqf	It is **better not to stop here**, due to a grammatical link with the next verse. However, due to it being the end of a verse, it is **permissible to stop**, and the meaning will remain sound. If the reciter stops, they will not repeat the kalimah mawqūfah when resuming recitation.
س سَكْتَه	السَّكْت Subtle pause	This symbol denotes silence. The reciter should **stop without breaking breath**, and then continue. **The saktah is compulsory in 4 places.**
وَقْفَه	الوَقْف مَعَ السَّكْت Longer pause	This symbol indicates longer pause than a 'saktah'. Again, the reciter **stops without breaking breath**, and then continues. A normal waqf can also be made here.
وَقْفُ النَّبِيّ	Pause of the Prophet ﷺ	This is where the Prophet ﷺ stopped; scholars have mentioned 11 places where this occurs. It is **preferable to stop** here.

وَقْف مُنَزَّل	وَقْف جبرائيل Pause of Jibrā᾽īl عليه السلام	This is where Angel Jibrā᾽īl عليه السلام paused at the time of revelation. It is **preferable to stop** here.
وَقْف غُفْرَان	Pause of forgiveness	This symbol indicates where the reciter and listener should stop to make du῾ā᾽. It is **preferable to stop** here.
وَقْف كُفْرَان	Pause of disbelief	This symbol indicates where stopping could create an incorrect meaning that could lead to kufr (disbelief). It is **strongly advised not to stop** here.

1) When reciting with **taḥqīq**, the reciter should stop on all the permitted stops. When reciting with **ḥadr**, the reciter should only stop on the required stops, unless there is a need to stop elsewhere. When reciting with **tadwīr**, the reciter should stop at the strong symbols, e.g. م ج ط and do waṣl at the weak ones, e.g. ز ص ق.

2) Stopping at impermissible places will not result in sin if the stopping was not made with a bad intention; in such a case, the reciter must resume the recitation by repeating a word from a suitable place.

3) An observant listener will find that reciters who are well-versed in the meaning of the Qur᾽ān might stop where there are no symbols, or continue at a stop symbol.

This is because they are able to determine if the meaning is corrupted by making waqf/waṣl in these places; remember, only knowledgeable reciters are able to do this.

Please note that there are differences in opinion amongst the scholars regarding the placement of symbols in certain places. Also, not all copies of the Qur᾽ān will contain all of the above symbols.

Appendix 5: Translations of the Qurʾān in other languages

It is not permissible to publish, sell, purchase or distribute a translation of the Qurʾān without the Arabic text. This is the unanimous view of the jurists and is the agreed position of the four schools of thought.

Muftī Taqi Uthmani writes in his *Contemporary Fatawa*:

'Ulama (scholars) have clarified that it is not allowed in Shari'ah to print or publish the translation of the Holy Quran without its Arabic text. It may be observed that the people of other religions have allowed to publish the translation of their Holy books without their original text and consequently the translations have spread so widely that the original text was ignored and it is not available today. In order to avoid such consequences it was held by the Muslim jurists that the translation of the Holy Quran should always be accompanied by the Arabic text of the Holy book.

(...)If somebody goes through such translations he may have the reward of studying the Holy Quran yet the reward specified for its recitation cannot be achieved except by reciting the original text of it.'

Please note that there may be scope to quote the translation of one or two verses of the Qurʾān without mentioning the Arabic, as long as the audience is not under illusion that the translation is part of the actual Qurʾān. For example, a writer may word their sentence thus: 'Allah SWT mentions in verse 45 of Sūrat al-Kahf, the translation of which is...'

However, it is best to practice caution in this matter and quote the Arabic text where possible.

Appendix 6: Divisions in the Qur᾿ān

Key words

Word	Meaning
sūrah (plural – suwar)	chapter
āyah (plural – āyāt)	verse
rukūʿ (plural – rukūʿāt)	sūrah section or 'paragraph'
ḥizb (plural – aḥzāb)	juz᾿ section (Arabian muṣḥaf)
juz᾿ (plural – ajzā᾿)	part
manzil (plural – manāzil)	stopping place
makkīyah	a chapter in which the majority of verses were revealed in Makkah
madanīyah	a chapter in which the majority of verses were revealed in Madīnah

Divisions in the 13-line Qur᾿ān

The Qur᾿ān consists of 114 suwar; each one is made up of a number of āyāt. Each sūrah is divided into a number of rukūʿāt, each of which contain verses that generally deal with one topic.

The Qur᾿ān is also divided into 30 equal ajzā᾿ for ease of recitation. Each juz᾿ is divided into 4 parts, marked in the margins as follows: الرُّبْع – end of first quarter, النِّصْف – end of half, الثَّلَاثَة – end of third quarter.

When given a quarter to recite, conventional practice is for the reciter to continue reading after the quarter symbol, until the end of the rukūʿ.

The rukūʿ symbol

The symbol denoting the end of a rukūʿ is an ع in the margin of a page. It has 3 numerical values attached to it: the top number denotes the position of the rukūʿ within the sūrah, the middle number shows how many verses it contains, and the bottom one denotes its position within the juzʾ.

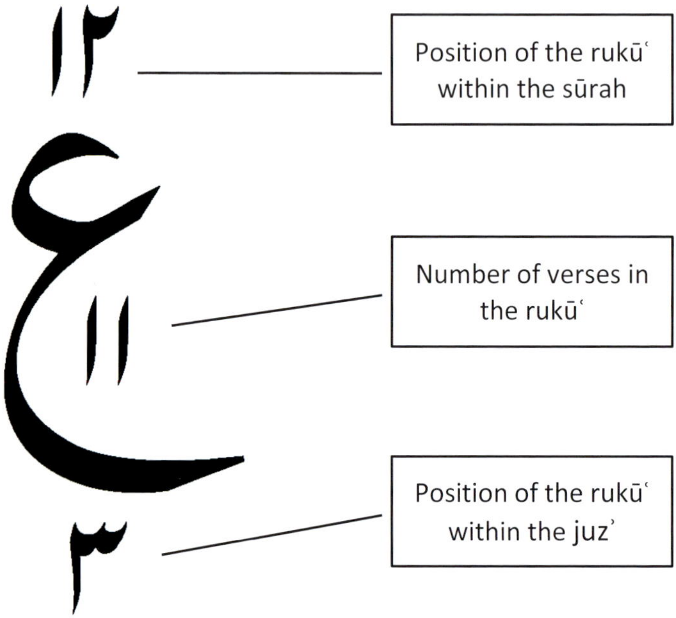

The ʿArabī muṣḥaf

In the Arabian muṣḥaf, each juzʾ is divided into 2 equal aḥzāb, each in turn divided into 4 equal parts. This makes a total of 8 small parts in each juzʾ, which are marked in the margin and the text.

The sūrahs themselves are not divided into sections.

The seven manāzil

For those who wish to complete one Qur'ān within a week, they may recite according to the seven manāzil. This is taken from the practice of the ṣaḥābah ﷺ:

Manzil No.	Sūrahs recited	No. of sūrahs	Juz' No.
1	الفَاتِحَة (١) – النِّسَاء (٤)	1 + 3	1 - 6
2	المائدَة (٥) – التَّوْبَة (٩)	5	6 - 11
3	يُوْنُس (١٠) – النَّحل (١٦)	7	11 - 14
4	الإسْرَاء (١٧) – الفُرْقَان (٢٥)	9	15 - 19
5	الشُّعَرَاء (٢٦) – يٰس (٣٦)	11	19 - 23
6	الصّٰفّٰت (٣٧) – الحُجُرَات (٤٩)	13	23 - 26
7	قٓ (٥٠) – النَّاس (١١٤)	The rest (65)	26 - 30

These are marked in the 13-line muṣḥaf in the bottom or side margins.

Bibliography

Arabic - books

Al-Muktafā fi ‘l-Waqf wal-Ibtidā fī Kitābi ‘llah ‘azza wa jall – Al-Imām Abū ‘Amr ‘Uthmān ibn Sa‘īd ad-Dānī al-Andalusi, Mu’assat ar-Risālah (Beirut)

An-Nashr fi ‘l-Qirā’āt al-‘Ashr – Al-Ḥāfiẓ Muḥammad ibn Muḥammad ad-Dimashqī (Ibn al-Jazarī), Dār al-Kutub al-‘Ilmīyah (Beirut)

At-Tajwīd Al-Muṣawwar – Doctor Ayman Rushdī Suwayd, Dār al-Ghawthāni li ‘d-Dirāsāt al-Qur’ānīyah (Damascus)

Ḥaqq at-Tilāwah – Ḥusnī Shaykh ‘Uthmān, Maktabat al-Manār (Az-Zarqā’, Jordan)

Arabic – video

abd Arachid al djannah (2012), مخارج الحروف العربية كلها لفضيلة الشيخ أيمن رشدي سويد. Available at: https://www.youtube.com/watch?v=0TSC5XUmIgE (Accessed 30 June 2016)

abd Arachid al djannah (2013), صفات الحروف كلها للشيخ الدكتور ايمن رشدي سويد. Available at: https://www.youtube.com/watch?v=ipi1oGSTEGA (Accessed 30 June 2016)

Umm Abdullah (2013), معنى تعريف الإخفاء.. و حقيقة الإخفاء الشفوي.. Available at: https://www.youtube.com/watch?v=2ThJXEBOnvI (Accessed 30 June 2016)

Alaa Ragab (2013), الشبهة التى ردها الشيخ أيمن سويد بعد 20 سنة بخصوص عمل الفرجة عند الاخفاء الشفوى والاقلاب. Available at: https://www.youtube.com/watch?v=Pims9WmhN5Y (Accessed 30 June 2016)

الشيخ أيمن رشدي (2011), احمد عبدالحميد سويد. – احكام التجويد –الامالة. Available at: https://www.youtube.com/watch?v=0pYaBOXIJo (Accessed 13 March 2017)

Umm Abdullah (2015), المنظومة الجزريّة كاملة.. بصوت الشّيخ أيمن سويد. Available at: https://www.youtube.com/watch?v=VRSjxLxY-7Q (Accessed 13 March 2017)

English

A Comprehensive Guide to Tajweed – Muawiyah ibn (Mufti) Abdus-Samad, Jamiatul Ilm Wal Huda (Blackburn)

Urdu

Al-Jawāhir an-Naqīyah fī Sharḥ al-Muqaddmat al-Jazarīyah – Qāri’ Iẓhār Aḥmad Thānvī, Maktabah Ishā‘at at-Tajwīd (Lahore)

Fawā’id Makkīyah – Qāri’ ‘Abd ar-Raḥmān Makkī, Khurshīd Book Depot (Lucknow)

Jamāl al-Qur’ān – Mawlāna Ashraf ‘Alī Thānvī, Educational Press (Karachi)

Rawḍat at-Tajwīd – Qāri’ Zakirhusen, Darul Uloom Al Arabiya Al Islamiya (Bury)